MADELENE ALLEN

REUNION
The Search for
My Birth Family

Published in 1992 by
Stoddart Publishing Co. Limited
34 Lesmill Road
Toronto, Canada
M3B 2T6

Canadian Cataloguing in Publication Data

Allen, Madelene C.
Reunion : the search for my birth family

ISBN 0-7737-2588-1

1. Allen, Madelene C.   2. Birthparents - Canada -
Identification.   3. Adoptees - Canada - Biography.
HV874.82.A5A3 1992   362.82'98'092   C92-093080-8

Typesetting: Tony Gordon Ltd.
Printed and bound in Canada

*To my three families
and to the memory of my adoptive parents and of
my birth father, whom I never knew but whose
character lives through his family in their love.*

*"Thank you and Parent Finders, so very much, for
the big part you played in bringing our two families
together. It has been an unbelievable, happy time for
us all. Why must it be such a difficult procedure? I
realize that not all such reunions are happy ones, nor
long-lasting, as I know ours is going to be, but there
must be ways of anticipating the problem ones. . . .
Ours — we wanted the whole world to know. . . ."*

— Letter from my birth mother to Parent Finders,
August, 1985

CONTENTS

PREFACE

*Adoption is like an elephant in the corner
which everyone effects not to notice.*
Erica Haimes and Noel Timms,
Adoption, Identity, and Social Policy

W E ARE LIVING in an era of heightened awareness of individual rights, and yet there is a hidden minority of several hundred thousand Canadians who have no access to their original birth certificates and family medical records. Adult adoptees are living in a personal historical void. Those of us who were adopted have faced the challenges of childhood, adolescence and adulthood, all the while carrying that extra piece of baggage labelled ADOPTED. For some of us it was never a burden. For others, it was an awkward weight, which slowed us down and made our steps unsure. The quandary in which we find ourselves stems not from a wish to choose between parents but from a wish to know our background, our heritage.

Our minority status as adult adoptees is not based on any psychological or physical condition but simply on the fact that at some time in our infancy or childhood we were given to others to be raised "as if born" to them. We are those whom P.D. James, in her novel *Innocent Blood*, has described as "displaced persons whose umbilical cord was a court order." Adoption is, without a doubt, a sensitive topic, for many lives and family relationships are bound up in the system that decreed that a child could be passed from one family to another in legal secrecy.

This book is a plea for understanding and for action. It was conceived in joy and confusion and fuelled by a certain amount of anger.

My joy at the successful conclusion to my four years of intensive searching was profound. I wanted to write about it, to give hope and perhaps some direction to other searching adoptees. Perhaps this book will also counter some of the loneliness and guilt that go hand in hand with an adoption search.

The confusion I experienced was a natural outcome of the readjustment of my social being. A new and accepting family has come into my life and a whole new set of relationships is there waiting to be sorted out: a happy situation, but confusing.

And the anger? I was never angry at my birth parents, for they were victims of the society of the early 1940s; nor was my anger focussed on my adoptive parents, for they, too, were caught up in the philosophy of secrecy that was inherent in the whole adoption procedure. My anger was, and is, directed against the state and a society that fostered this conspiracy of silence and secrecy, which envelops not only the adoptee, but both sets of parents. We, the adoptees, have also been culpable. We have lacked the courage to ask questions, and we have been unwilling to face the complexity of guilt that made us accomplices to the conspiracy. It is only by speaking out that we can make society aware of our very particular circumstances.

As I progressed with my research, I began to see the book as a celebration, touching the three sides of the adoption triangle. It is a celebration of the strength of our birth parents who, because of the mores of a society, made the decision (or perhaps had it made for them) to cut all ties with their own flesh and blood. It is a celebration of the courage of people who take an infant or young child into their lives, and who love that child as their own. And we adoptees, the third side of the triangle, also have cause to celebrate — for we can come to a deeper understanding of the importance and love of families by accepting the challenge to delve into our past, or even by deciding to accept the status quo.

I hope this book will help anyone involved in the adoption triangle personally or professionally, and all those who are interested in this modern drama, this human search that leads to reunion.

ACKNOWLEDGEMENTS

My thanks to . . .

My birth family, for their understanding and willingness to be central characters, and to all those who helped me to find them!

The staff of Camp Ouareau, 1990, whose skill allowed me the time needed to write in the midst of summer. A special "yo!" to Jacqui Raill, my assistant director, and program director Nara Stockwell.

Arnold Edinborough, who believed in the book.

Charles Marquette and Nicole Mohr, who donated their time to search out elusive Quebec information and addresses.

Cynthia Strong for sharing her thesis.

Joan Buchanan and the members of our writing group in Sherbrooke, Quebec, for their encouragement.

Jean Levesque and Judy Humphreys, who read the manuscript at a vital time.

The representatives of the Child and Family Support Services, Post-Adoption, of the provinces, who sent information and answered questions.

I also learned that the need to complete a self-image by discovering the truth about the past is not confined to any one social or economic class, nor does a desire to know one's natural parents have anything to do with childhood happiness or unhappiness. This desire is simply a human need more evident in some individuals than others. Yet adoptees are the only group prevented by law from satisfying this need. The records of their births and adoptions are sealed.

If we prize conscience, memory, and history, we should welcome a revival of a basic freedom. This freedom is not new or novel. The prohibition against finding the truth is an aberration.

Henry Ehrlich, A Time to Search

1

HOW IT ALL BEGAN

Anyone can live with the truth, no one
can live with lies and only those who live
a lie can appreciate the difference.
Joss Shawyer, *Death by Adoption*

M Y NEED TO search for my birth parents came from a lesson deeply instilled in my soul by my adoptive parents: the importance of one's ancestry. As a child, growing up in Toronto, I watched my father and uncle poring over documents and family trees to trace a Scottish relative born in 1730. In 1957 my adoptive parents took me, a gangling fifteen-year-old, to Scotland, where we visited my great-great-grandfather's grave in Balquidder. The old church where he married my great-great-grandmother stands in ruins beside the "new" church. Moss-covered gravestones mark the passage of generations. I have been drawn back a number of times, and over my desk today hang photographs of that hauntingly beautiful Highland valley. I can tell you the name of the ship on which they emigrated, and trace their path to a pioneer farmstead in western Ontario. As for more recent family history, my father took me to walk his battlefields of Passchendaele and Vimy Ridge. I will never forget his profound silence as we stood on that piece of Canadian soil and looked over the plain towards Lens. He returned to Canada in 1919, finished high school and entered medicine, and spent his life working for the Department of Veterans' Affairs. He never spoke of the war, but the focus of his life spoke more vividly than words ever could of the impact that his experiences in the trenches had had on his life.

My mother's family emigrated from Germany in the last years of the nineteenth century and, as happened in so many loyal Canadian families of German extraction during the First World War, the family's European history was buried, never to resurface. My father's family was my only link to my European past and perhaps this is why I felt so strongly about my Scottish heritage.

Long summer evenings were spent in front of a log fire blazing in the great stone fireplace of a Muskoka cabin. Coal oil lamps cast their gentle glow on the log walls, pushing darkness into the far corners. After the whip-poorwill ceased its nightly concert, the howl of timber wolves would often echo from hill to hill. I sat entranced by the stories woven by my grandfather, uncle, aunt and parents in those days before television. My parents (as I will refer to my adoptive parents) were a great deal older than most parents, and my grandfather was born in 1865. He would tell vibrant, vivid stories of William Lyon McKenzie King, of the Boer War, of St. Elmo's fire, of swamp gas and devils, and of the Black Donnellys. Family history and pioneer pride were woven into my very being, as was pride in my family.

The great-aunts and cousins would gather on the hollyhock porch when we came to visit my mother's family in a tiny western Ontario town. They and my parents are now gathered in the hillside graveyard, their voices distant memories, but forty years ago the laughter and gossip settled in the subconscious of a small girl who wasn't really listening. The odd phrase lingered and these memories wove themselves together into an impression that there was something different about our family. There was no particular event, no specific revelation or incident that I can now remember that gave me this feeling. It has been observed that the invisible antennae of adopted children are longer than those of "natural" children. We don't know what we don't know, but we know there is something that we aren't supposed to know and that that something is at the very foundation of our being. After the revelation of the fact of adoption has been made to a child, there is so much more she wants to know — most of all, *why*. Childhood ears grow large hoping to pick up clues about the past from the gossiping conversations of their elders.

I am now delving back forty years, to summertime days on the edge of that tiny, sleepy village in western Ontario. These were days to roller-skate down the single main street to the library, which was tucked into a claustrophobic room above the town offices. Days to watch the clock moving towards the magic hour of 3:30, so I could run through the fragrant fields at the back of my great-aunt's property to watch the steam train chugging its way from Wingham to Goderich. The weekdays crept by until Friday afternoon when my father would come from Toronto and we could walk, hand in hand, to the newspaper office, where he would buy a copy of the weekly newspaper for himself and a new colouring book for me. The smell of printer's ink still brings back the vision of that tiny wood-lined office, the counter impossibly high for a young child who wanted to watch the typesetter hunched over his table painstakingly setting up next week's issue. I would peer around the corner of that great wooden wall, and sometimes he would notice me and invite me to join him in his sanctum, where I could stand beside him and watch. Sundays meant church with peppermints and crinkly paper, and afterwards all the uncles, aunts, cousins, assorted friends, maiden ladies and old bachelors of the village sitting around a vast farm table laden with the glorious food that can only come from German kitchens. Then my father would be gone for another five days.

A child's mind is alive; for some imaginative children there are fantasies, but all children wonder about the past and the future. For adoptees, there is the realization of being "different": relatives watching to see family traits, interests; the child herself trying to be interested in the things her parents are interested in, trying always to please them. One of my clearest childhood memories is people saying to me, "My, you look just like your mother," or "How you take after your father." I always wanted to say to the first remark, "No, I don't, I'm adopted," and to the second, "Only because I want to." I suppose even at such tender years I knew that such things were "just not done," for I grew up in a day and age, and in a family, where the "done" and the "not done" were very important; it became a code for right and wrong, the acceptable and the unacceptable, and I couldn't risk breaking the rules.

I was living in two worlds. I was part of my adoptive family, and without any hesitation took their heritage and history as my own. On the other hand, once I knew that I was adopted, the secrecy that surrounded this fact made me wonder passionately about my real heritage. There were such fascinating stories about ancestors in this family that I could not help wondering about the stories of the people whose blood flowed in *my* veins.

My dearly loved parents are dead, for as in the case of so many adoptive parents they were much older than "normal" parents. This was considered in those days to be a positive thing. I was brought up by parents who were in their forties when I joined the family, and thus they were in their sixties when I was a teenager. They had been born at the turn of the century: their values and attitudes were very different from those of my friends' parents, and vastly different from those that began to be current in the fifties and sixties, when I was struggling with my own growth and social development. My friends' parents had at least grown up in the twenties, a period in which the constraints of the strait-laced post-Victorian era were cast aside. Any difficulties I encountered in my growing up stemmed from this fundamental difference.

Like any only child, I was lonely without a brother or sister. My mother only laughed when I asked her if I could have one. I remember an ad on one of the Toronto radio stations in the late 1940s advertising an automobile dealership called Ted Davy: "Try Ted Davy, Ted Davy, Ted Davy." I thought the man with the deep voice was singing: "Buy a baby, a baby, a baby." It was unfair, so many of my friends had brothers and sisters. Why couldn't I? I remember declaring to my mother that if I could have only one child when I grew up, I would adopt another, because it wasn't fair being an only child. I can't remember if I knew, at the time, that I was adopted. I think not. How that must have hurt her — but on the other hand, what a marvellous opening it would have given her, had she chosen to take it!

I don't know exactly how old I was when the revelation was made to me — perhaps seven or eight. However, the scene is as vivid in my memory as if it happened yesterday.

My mother called me into their bedroom and handed me a book. I loved books and the thought of a new one to read filled me with joy. The bedroom was green — the bedspread was a soft gray-green satin, and drapes of the same material hung in elegant folds on either side of sun-filled windows. I lay down on the bed (where else does a child read a book, except perhaps on the floor?) and my mother left the room.

The binding of that little book was red. I hope that all such books have been burned. It presented a lovely young couple wandering up and down a row of bassinets, each containing a tiny, perfect infant. After due deliberation, akin to the consideration one might give to a litter of puppies, they pointed: *That one, please.* I was "that one" — I was the best, I had been chosen. The writer didn't touch on where we had all come from, we perfect babes in a row, or what we were doing until these wonderful people, who didn't look in the least like my parents, came to get us; or what happened to the unlucky souls who weren't chosen. Nor did the writer consider why these people were looking at all. My idea of where babies came from was hazy enough at that age, but I did know they weren't found under gooseberry bushes, or picked from rows of little bassinets!

My mother's leaving the room indicated her attitude to adoption, and set the tone for the future. The memory of that exit said, "Don't ask, don't even consider it. I will never talk about it." I didn't realize the full implications of her action at that time, of course, but I had gotten the message, and I never questioned her about my adoption. I wonder now how it must have been for her, always wondering when and if this rather precocious child would bring up the forbidden topic. We were always able to communicate well over the years, except for that one barrier.

My mother was a good, kind woman, with a gentle heart and a strong backbone, but she could not bear unpleasantness or confrontation. She gave me her love, but she could never give me what would have cemented a very special relationship: honesty in that one thing, which mattered so much. My mother was scrupulously honest and upright in every other way. My parents gave me a warm and caring home, a love of good books and music, a private school education, summer camp; they gave me gifts from the heart, not the least of which was their time (how can I ever forget the hours my mother spent drilling me in spelling, and in French verbs?). She gave me my love of classical music — as a child I would lie in bed while she played me to sleep with Chopin, Mozart and Beethoven. Most importantly, they gave me their love and support through my tempestuous growing-up years, and later as I branched out to make my own life. I know her reactions were influenced by her circumstances. My mother herself was the only child of a much older, traditional Victorian woman. I knew my grandmother well; she lived with my parents until she died, and thus had a great influence on my upbringing. She was born in 1880, and so it's little wonder I had to battle some antiquated ideas, and even now I carry, as my cross, some of her attitudes — they are part of my very being. One of her favourite litanies involved having the courage of your convictions and standing up for what you believe in — little did she know where this lesson would lead her granddaughter! Not until death claimed her, at eighty-four, did this diminutive matriarch let her own child, my mother, go. With this background, how could my mother risk coping with the inevitable questions of a small child or blossoming teenager — questions with which she herself probably could not come to grips with in her own heart?

For many years I considered the fact that I was adopted as simply part of my identity — in much the same category as the fact that I had freckles and long braids. I never told anyone, not even my best friends; some instinct warned me that it was better not to. No youngster will ever deliberately open himself to the possibility of scorn or derision from his peers or even his best friends. Friendship is tenuous when you are young. Even to be seen as different is a risk.

I only once went through an intense period of discomfort and confusion. That was in grade school, as a result of the family tree exercise, that traditional favourite of teachers. I was quite happy drawing my tree, which went back further than those of most of my friends; but at the same time I remember feeling very uncomfortable. The names that I was putting on weren't really those of my ancestors, and yet they were. I can understand the confusion I felt then. Sadly, there was no one with whom I could discuss my dilemma.

Apart from this one event the whole subject lay relatively dormant in my mind until I was fourteen. In that year my father brought the subject up, in an oblique manner, on two occasions. These were the only times he ever referred to my adoption.

It was 1957, and we were planning our trip to Europe. I was very excited, and when the passport forms arrived, I felt truly independent as I filled in my own. My father looked over my shoulder as I sat at my desk, the papers spread out before me. He leaned down, pointed at the offending error and said, "Barrie, not Toronto."

He was gone from the room before I could react. In the space provided for place of birth I had written TORONTO, for that was what was on my birth certificate, but poor Dad, my honest, upright father, could not let me write something that was not true — even on a form that no one would ever make the effort to verify. And, if by any remote chance it was checked, the inspector would only find false information on a legal document. My original, accurate birth certificate is well and truly sealed in the depths of the Registrar General's office, never to see the light of day. The only birth certificate in the public record is the altered document.

Records are falsified at each step of the adoption process. I was not born in Toronto, and the names of the people on my birth certificate are not those of my birth parents. Recently, adoptive parents have complained that this practice is tantamount to fraud. If any business substituted names on a legal form, they would be breaking the law, but for some reason it is condoned on documents pertaining to an adopted child. Essentially it boils down to this: I carry false papers! (I wonder now what would happen if I applied with my birth name for a "replacement" birth certificate. Would I find that I do not exist?)

The second time was before a father-daughter ski trip with a colleague and his daughter. My father commented casually, as we were gathering our equipment, that he knew "girls talked" and I was not to mention being adopted. How bizarre! I had never spoken of it, he had never spoken of it, so why would he think he had to mention it under these circumstances? Many years later I realized that his friend, with whom we were going skiing, was the doctor who delivered me. Did Dad think that his friend's daughter would know, or was he afraid that I would mention it in front of everyone and that the dear doctor would have let the cat out of the bag?

The spectre of my past reared its head during my youth on several occasions without the fact of adoption itself being mentioned. The incident I remember most vividly, which I now see was related to my parents' fears about adoption, occurred when I was in university. I had been involved in the drama club throughout my college years. In my final year I had the opportunity to try out for the lead in the main play, *The Good Woman of Setzuan*. The casting was to be immediately after the Christmas holidays. Full of expectation and hope, I brought the script home to prepare for the final audition. Two days before my return, my father picked up the script and read the play. He then quietly informed me that I was not to try out. The main character was a prostitute, and he would not allow his daughter on stage in the role of a fallen woman. He had missed the whole point of the play. He was only concerned with what people would think. I ranted and raved, but he would not relent. I was twenty years of age, lived away from home in residence — and I obeyed him! The bitterness has stayed with me, but also the anger at myself for being so spineless. Yet, there was just too much baggage attached to my relationship with my parents for me to disobey them. I loved my father, and I respected him, and even at that age would not go against his wishes. I couldn't help wondering, after the initial anger had subsided, if there was not more to his action. Had my mother been a prostitute? Did he assume that since I was adopted I was probably illegitimate, and therefore any link with anything smacking of immorality would cast an even more suspicious light on my character?

It wasn't until A.M. McWhinnie's study, *Adopted Children — How They Grow Up*, was published in 1966 that any connection was made between the levels of discomfort felt by the adopters and their adopted children. This study pointed out that children raised in an atmosphere of openness about their adoption tend not to ask questions, whereas those who are brought up with secrecy have an intense desire to know the facts. The study also pointed out that "the more loyal and loving the child, the fewer questions he would be likely to ask." Joss Shawyer, the author of *Death by Adoption*, confirms that mine was not an unusual case. She observed:

Adopted people have been made to feel that to want to know about themselves will be hurtful to others. And so we have this extraordinary situation where children are forced to keep their most basic feelings about themselves hidden from their parents so their parents don't get hurt. . . . Adopted children denied knowledge of themselves have lonely childhoods protecting their parents from reality and being unable to express their deepest feelings about themselves to the very people who should be able to listen and encourage such confidences.

A number of factors were involved in the reluctance of my parents to bring up the topic, and perhaps even to face it themselves. They had probably been counselled to put the whole manner of my entrance into the family behind them and to treat me as truly their own. It was a secrecy that was closely tied to the stigma of unmarried parenthood. A child placed for adoption was usually born out of wedlock, a "poor wee thing" doomed to be raised in an orphanage unless some kind souls took her into their home. The stigma of infertility also played a part. If a family adopted it meant that "something was wrong" with one of them. This assumption alone threatened their self-esteem. The reaction of their families was often one of pity that they were in some way deficient, and that they were perhaps having to settle for second best. Thus, adoption reflected on them not only as individuals, but as parents coping with a whole set of unknown genes bound up in this new, tiny bundle of life. Is it any wonder that a couple would not broadcast their new arrival?

Adoption deals with the very basics of human love, loyalty, family life and self-esteem. Self-esteem not only of the adoptee, but also of the birth and adoptive parents. These are very delicate emotions. I never felt that I was second best, as some adoptees do, but I did feel that I had something to prove. I had to prove to my parents that I was everything they hoped for. I was a happy, joyful tom-boy, thus fulfilling my father's wish for the companion that every man wants, and I loved every minute of it. I can string a worm on a hook, and cast to the centre of a pond and land the trout; I can paddle a canoe, sail a boat, ride a horse; at one time I was a very good shot with a .22 target rifle. I was a "good" girl: I finished university, became a teacher and then ran my own business. I have a happy marriage and my husband and I have raised two successful children. I did it for my own satisfaction, of course, but I was also pleased to prove something to those shadowy judges who sat back wondering how "the poor wee thing" would turn out.

Illegitimacy is a social stigma that one cannot escape, but the psychological identity that comes from the child's knowledge of illegitimacy goes hand in hand with her social identity. Feeling that I was created during a casual contact between two people had left me with a deep sense of emptiness. My drive to succeed stemmed, I believe, directly from a sense that I had to begin a worthy history to pass on, to somehow blot out the irresponsible action that had created me. All through my childhood, my years as a student, even in my first job and the profession I chose (one that demands responsibility and great self-reliance) — at every step of the way I felt that I had to prove myself. This brought a lot of stress into my life. Those who are constantly trying to prove themselves are not always easy to work or live with. My past was a black hole, my children had knowledge of only half of their heritage. What sort of legacy had I to pass on to them? None, except what I myself might do with my life.

Even though it was wartime, when marriages were often expeditious and brief affairs overlooked, there was still a strong, though contradictory, moral code. Divorce was frowned upon. Even in the sixties, children I knew at the summer camp I run would go to great lengths to hide the fact that they had divorced parents. Sex outside of marriage was taboo — indeed two people living together without marriage were considered to be "living in sin" — but now children speak comfortably of "daddy's girlfriend" who has just moved in. If a woman was foolish enough to "get herself pregnant" in the 1940s she was rejected by society and left to her own devices, unless she was scooped up by one of the various charitable or church groups and sent to await the happy event in a "home for wayward girls," or discreetly shipped off to the family farm or a distant relative so as not to bring any further disgrace upon her family. There was no question at that time of an unmarried woman bringing up a child born out of wedlock, unless, of course, the man involved did "the decent thing by her" and married her. The pregnant girl went through with her nine months and then in most cases gave up the child for adoption, either willingly or on the strong advice of well-meaning social workers. Society had not progressed philosophically very far beyond Hester Prynne's tribulations in Nathaniel Hawthorne's *The Scarlet Letter*. Birth control was not openly discussed, and methods were limited; indeed, it was illegal to sell condoms in Ontario until 1969. Termination of pregnancy was limited to old wives' practices or back-room abortionists. It was commonly believed that the sins of the fathers would reappear in the child, and the adoptive family was watched to see how "the child" would turn out. Birth and placement were over, finished with, history for both of my families. However, it was not over, it was my present.

The term "as if born" is used legally and the concept of the child belonging to the adoptive family is strong. Perhaps in the eyes of the law it *is* that simple; perhaps also in the hearts of the adoptive family, because they want it to be true. It may also be true for the adopted child some of the time, perhaps for a lifetime; but it is not true for all of us. As Kahlil Gibran wrote in *The Prophet*: "Your children are not your children. They are the sons and daughters of Life's longing for itself." I *am* part of the family that gave me my psychological upbringing, my nurturing; I am part of them by love, by shared experiences. However, as became eminently clear when I met my birth family, I also share a great deal with my biological family. The heredity-versus-environment debate takes on a very personal meaning for an adoptee.

Search for identity is all part of growing up. The adoptee does not wish to throw off, but to discover. Family expectations are not less for an adopted child, though they are sometimes less realistic. In many cases the expectations of adoptive parents are higher, more ambitious and more emphatically stated than those of natural parents. My adoptive mother was a concert pianist, and I studied piano diligently. I love music, but had little talent. Perhaps if I had been a "natural" child, I might have excelled and pleased her or, more accurately, pleased my grandmother.

Some adopted children fear that their security within the family is dependent on their ability to please their parents. My parents would never have put conditions on their love for me, but children's fears and attitudes are not always reasonable. It is impossible not to wonder if you are measuring up to the expectations your parents had when they chose you, no matter what your age. Fortunately my adoptive parents never said "after all we did for you," but somehow there was always the idea implanted deep in my mind that I must achieve, I must succeed so that I would not let my adoptive parents down. These thoughts are particularly heavy for an adoptee who has failed in an endeavour. I was devastated when in my last year of high school I failed French and had to repeat grade thirteen because of this one subject. The anticipated reaction of my parents worried me far more than the lost year. Their reaction? One of support and sorrow that they hadn't helped me more!

Children who are growing up adopted live their lives on two planes, one within the family they have and the other in a shadowy speculative "family" in their minds. Even though I was not an imaginative child I remember wondering where I would be if I had not been adopted. What would my life be like if I were still with my "other parents." I never played with dolls, I hated dress-ups (I still do, which is a real difficulty for a camp director). I did not, and do not, like anything to do with "let's pretend." It struck too close to home, for during the whole of my childhood I was the foundation of a masquerade for a whole family.

I am left with a fundamental sadness about my parents, which goes deeper than the grief I felt after their deaths. Perhaps this is an inevitable part of life for those who are born to or join the families of much older parents. I am saddened by the fact that my parents never had the experience of being grandparents except to babies and toddlers. I know how happy it would have made them to watch our children grow up; to mark the life stages of their grandchildren through high school and university graduation, marriage and perhaps even the birth of the next generation. And my children's lives would have been the richer for the influence of grandparents.

My sadness stems also from the fact that I never got to know my parents as individuals, separate from their role as parents. Not long before my mother's death we shared a very moving experience when we worked together on the traditional candlelight music-and-poetry evening which marks the close of camp. It entails finding music which exactly fits the poetry that is being read at the same time. Timing and sensitivity to rhythms are crucial to effective presentation. In twenty years I have only found one other person with whom I work as well as I worked with my mother for that week of preparation. She left camp the day after and she was dead two weeks later. Had she lived, our relationship surely would have taken on a whole new dimension because we had shared something far deeper than a parent-child experience.

Given time, we probably could have spoken of the family and of my coming. Perhaps both Mom and Dad went to their graves wishing that they could have told me about the uniqueness of our family, and regretting that they had not found the courage to do so. I had never given them any indication that it mattered to me at all, so I was as much to blame as they were. I felt guilty about this for some time after their deaths (eight years apart), and my guilt was only slightly assuaged when I read that it is natural for the adopted child to want information but to be reticent about asking for it.

Did I lose something very special, or did silence preserve our family?

2

THE REAL WORLD

*Today's sealed record controversy can not
be dismissed as simply the expression of a
few vocal dissidents. It must be viewed as
a moot issue. In this debate
open-mindedness is essential and such
open-mindedness has to include
consideration of the possibility that adult
adoptees may be right in demanding
elimination of secrecy.*

A.D. Sorosky, *The Adoption Triangle:
The Effect of Sealed Records*

WHAT IS IT that tips the scale and turns a satisfied adoptee, with only a natural interest in her situation, into someone obsessed with discovering the past? Every adoptee must wonder from time to time about her background, but it has been estimated that 70 percent of adoptees do not search. But given the increased interest in and awareness of the importance of background, and the number of participants in registries across the country, I doubt that figure. Even granting that only 30 percent of us do search, what is it that drives us to cross the line?

Very often it is a major life crisis or event that awakens the desire to search. It may be the death of an adoptive parent, the birth of a child, a divorce, or serious illness within the family. These are events that inevitably cause us to look deep into our souls.

When I held my daughter for the first time in 1968, I could not help thinking about the woman who had held me as a newborn. As I looked into that tiny face and dreamt the dreams of every new mother, I realized that even if this daughter of mine were spirited from me, I would never forget her. I could not imagine not knowing — ever — what had happened to her. How could I believe that a middle-aged woman, somewhere out there, had wiped me from her mind? As I nursed my child, the feeling grew stronger. I wanted that shadowy figure to know that I had had a happy life and was now a mother myself.

Our son was born two years later and my adoptive mother rejoiced in her grandchildren. When I saw the delight that my parents took in our two little ones I could not drive away the thought that that other woman might also like to know that she was the grandmother of two very special children. (Strangely, I did not wonder about my birth father in the same way, perhaps because the maternal bond was so immediate for me at that time.)

My mother died very suddenly in 1974, and within two years I had major back surgery, which left me severely limited in activity for the next four years. Perhaps I had far too much time to think, but more and more, the image of my birth mother and the darkness that was my past possessed my imagination. But I still was not seriously thinking of actually trying to find her.

My search, strangely enough, started by accident.

As the owner and director of a children's summer camp in Quebec, I travel several times each year to Ontario to interview staff and meet prospective campers. April 17, 1978, found me in Barrie, the town where I had been born thirty-six years before. I had come into town from the highway and was following carefully written directions to the home of our prospective camper. It was a beautiful spring day, the sun was streaming down, a warm breeze wafted from the hills. Like any stranger in a unfamiliar town, I had been gazing around me, enjoying the sights. The light turned red in front of me, offering a few moments when I did not have to concentrate on the traffic. There, to my left, was the hospital entrance. This was where I had been born! As if other hands were turning the wheel I manoeuvred across the traffic stream and found myself in the parking lot. "Is it worth asking?" I wondered. I had a few minutes before my appointment and, throwing caution to the winds, decided I would just ask for the birth records of July 3, 1942. No harm could come from a simple inquiry.

I stepped into the modern entrance hall and made my way through the corridors to the records office. Time was ticking away, and if the person in front of me had taken just two more minutes with his inquiry I would have had to leave. However, his question was dealt with very quickly, and there I was standing in front of the counter. The young clerk gazed up expectantly. In all innocence I asked whether it was possible to see a list of children born July 3, 1942. The woman smiled and very calmly said:

"You're adopted, aren't you?"

"Uh, yes."

"I'm sorry, I can't help you."

I stood there looking blank. The implication was that if I hadn't been adopted the files would have been opened.

"Why don't you go the Children's Aid?" she added helpfully.

I thanked her, and feeling like a perfect fool beat a hasty retreat. How on earth had she guessed? I was taken aback at her automatic assumption, but I might have just as well handed her a business card engraved with the words: MADELENE ALLEN, ADOPTEE. People simply don't walk in off the street and ask for a list of children born on a certain date thirty-six years before. If this information should be needed as part of a statistical survey, formal letters of explanation and questionnaires would be sent to the institution, and it would be the numbers which would be important, not the names. In the ensuing years I was to learn a great deal about how to find information and how to ask questions without revealing the obvious — how to be devious, in fact.

The interview with the family of the camper was not one of my better ones. My feelings were in turmoil — it was one of the few times I was not able to subordinate my personal life to my professional duties. Too much had happened too quickly, and I had been entirely unprepared.

As I drove out of Barrie, an anger was born in me, a smouldering anger that was to become the driving force of my search. I had been able to live with my dissatisfaction and unhappiness with family secrecy. That was the decision of my parents. I could not agree with their reasoning, but had felt that that was their right; I accepted their version of our life because it was theirs, and I had never felt strongly enough about wanting to know to risk precipitating a crisis. I had no desire to hurt or alienate my parents. Bureaucracy, however, was another matter. The rights of the individual under the Freedom of Information Act had been widely published and I had innocently thought that this applied to *all* personal information held by governments and institutions. But there, behind me in the hospital, my records were sitting silently amidst thousands of others. Other people's records could be had for the asking, but mine might as well have been thrown out or erased, for my name had disappeared into the shadowy world of sealed records. As a truck passed me, I suddenly realized that I didn't even know my own name! If I had been given a list of those born on July 3, 1942, I wouldn't have known which of the girls was me. Was there only one child born on that date? Were there five?

I was growing angrier by the minute. What harm would it have done to let me see the list? A list of names is not identifying information. Mary Smith, Jane Doe, Heather Whosit, Alleyne Attwood, our old summer-camp friend Agatha Clunchbucket — they were all the same to me at that stage, except that one of those names referred to the five-foot-six, short-brown-haired individual who was asking. The only conceivable reason why that information would be confidential was to stop an adoptee from seeing her original name, because that name could be just the clue that allowed her to initiate a search.

Sealed records are the glue that holds the adoption myth together. It is ironic, in this day and age of computers, when so much personal information is available so quickly and easily to so many people, that adoption records are still sealed. We leave a paper trail behind us as we progress through life — credit ratings, government records, medical records, driver's licences, school records, mortgage papers and finally our wills — all of which are available to any number of interested parties. Mail order houses and charitable institutions have our addresses and are free to pass them on, and on, and on. But for adoptees the records are locked away, inaccessible. (And this has not changed with current legislation.)

When I made that early, impulsive inquiry, I had given no thought at all to the importance of asking questions in the right way. I had not even seriously considered what the right questions might be, or whether I knew whom to ask. I later learned how very important it was to go to the appropriate people. If, for example, instead of going to the records department I had gone to the social services department of the Barrie hospital, they might have given me more constructive advice.

My inquiry at the hospital had gotten me nowhere, but it marked an important step in my gradual realization that I *was* going to search for my birth family. Although I couldn't have articulated it at the time, I was growing more and more convinced that if I was ever to be a whole person I had to know the facts of my heritage.

For each individual there is such a turning point. Some may feel, after a rebuff, that the search will be too hard on them emotionally, and they will not continue. Others, more convinced of the rightness of the goal, will press on. If for me the turning point had come at the end of summer, with a long winter stretching before me, I might have followed up these feelings of anger and frustration and started a full-blown search right away. However, the period from April to September is the most hectic time for a camp director, and when fall came the moment had passed. One incident and the ensuing few hours of thought on the drive home had not created a commitment strong enough to survive the summer. The current of my life took over again. My children were small, and the political situation in Quebec resulted in a great exodus of English families, and thus campers, from the province; for the next three years all my energies were focussed on my business, my family, and (not the least of my problems) coping with a bad back.

The years rolled by, my children grew into responsible human beings, the camp filled again as we developed a bilingual program and life became much calmer and more ordered. Still, I did nothing to pick up the lines of thought which had been so earth-shaking thirty-nine months before.

Then, one summer morning in July, 1981, the ground shifted again under my feet.

Radios are not a part of our camp world. The reception is poor in the mountains, and we are simply too busy on our own little planet to worry about happenings in the mad outside world. However, for some reason one was on in the room next to my office — perhaps some staff member was making a poster or drawing up lists, and wanted some distraction. I had been moving back and forth between the two rooms. Suddenly, the word *adoption* came booming out from what had been quiet background chatter. I mumbled apologies, unceremoniously unplugged the radio and retreated quickly with it to the peace of the inner office, after telling my secretary that unless there was a crisis of major proportions (lost T-shirts and a confused day-off schedule did not count), she was to hold the fort and not let anyone come near me until I re-emerged.

CBC's "Morningside" was broadcasting an interview with a representative from Parent Finders. That program changed my life, clichéd as that may sound. There were more out there like me, *many* more. Adoptees had actually banded together to help one another. I wasn't strange or abnormal for wanting to know about my past. For the first time in my eleven years of directing a camp I honestly, truly, wished I could send all one hundred children home so I could get on with my search. Search? What search? Was I going to search? Yes! In the course of that half hour it had suddenly become possible, and even inevitable. There were ways and means, and I now had a vehicle to find out what they were. But I would have to wait six weeks until the last bus disappeared down the road, until the last report was filed. Even though I would have to put this drive into my subconscious while I got on with the business at hand — seeing a hundred youngsters through a happy, safe, fun-filled summer — I knew that this time my determination was real.

I learned two important things from that radio interview. First, that I knew almost nothing about the adoption process. I had never even heard of an adoption order, the document that gives the adoptive parents all the legal rights of parents; it is the court order that passes the child from the birth family to the adoptive family. This document cuts you off forever from your roots, unless your adoptive parents choose to share the information contained therein with you. It is available to the adult adoptee — as long as the adoptee can produce proof of the adoptive parents' death or has written permission from them if they are alive. This requirement seemed to me to be absolutely unbelievable . . . that *adults* would need their parents' written permission to get a document. We are adults, perhaps parents ourselves, but in the eyes of the law, we are still children. It is a shocking situation for an adult to be put into: having to wait until parents — whom we love, and who gave us a home, love, nurturing — are permanently out of our lives before we can obtain a basic document. My father was still alive, and so I had to wait. Asking him for permission to apply for my adoption order was simply not an option. I knew I couldn't do it. I thought that in all likelihood he had the original buried in his papers, but I never considered going through them to find it. When I sorted out his things after his death I expected to find it, but I was disappointed. At some stage he must have destroyed it.

Second, I learned that I could apply to the Children's Aid Society for my non-identifying information. This is the compilation of all the information that an anonymous social worker deems it safe for an adoptee to know about her past. The social worker gleans from the files those few tantalizing tidbits that give the adoptee information about her ethnic heritage, family situation and certain parental characteristics. This information is edited so that nothing is included that might identify the place of birth, the names of the birth family — anything, in short, that could give the reader a clue to identity.

For some reason I had it firmly fixed in my mind that I needed to know my birth name before I could apply to the Children's Aid Society for my non-identifying information, and consequently I did nothing at the time. I cannot imagine why I thought so, for with even a moment's reflection I would have realized that their files must be cross-referenced under both birth and adoptive names. Until my father died and I obtained my adoption order, I put action on hold. Had I written then and there, months could have been saved, for the list of requests for non-identifying information was growing longer by the week. But I had less time to wait than I expected, for in March, 1981, my father died after a long illness.

I was filled with grief, but with his death came a feeling of release. I was freed from the sense of debt that is natural for many adoptive children, and I prayed that at some future time I would also be released from the profound sense of guilt that accompanied my desire to search. This unfortunately was not to be, for I still feared that I would be seen as an ungrateful adoptee. I was afraid that family friends would consider my search for my birth parents, after the death of my adoptive parents, as not only unseemly but also proof that I did not truly love them, and that I was an unworthy member of the family. Self-esteem is so very closely bound up with how we think others perceive us, that it would be some time before I could come to grips with these fears, and it was only with the support of some of my parents' closest friends that I realized they were totally unfounded. The atmosphere of secrecy within the home had given me these feelings of guilt and I was both amazed and surprised when I found that they did not think that way. Almost without exception the family and our friends understood my need to know, supported me whole-heartedly and wished me Godspeed on my quest.

My father was buried beside my mother in the quiet rural graveyard on a blustery day in March during an early spring snowstorm. It seemed appropriate — so many of his stories had centred on the farm and snow. As we stood waiting for the last of the cars to arrive at the graveyard, I remembered the strong, handsome man he had been. I thought of his stories of riding his old horse to school in the early morning to start the fires, or of the farmer lost in the whiteout between the house and the barn.

However, as we drove homeward, I knew, with relief, that I was now free to start my search in earnest; nothing stood in the way. I could apply for the documents I needed, which were available "on the death of the adoptive parents."

Getting the copy of my adoption order was at the head of my list. I knew that once I had my birth name, I could get my non-identifying information. To secure the adoption order, I had to apply to the Ministry of Community and Social Services of Ontario, in Toronto. Under the impression that getting it would be akin to taking a book out of the library, I decided to go to the office in person, to save time.

I arrived in Toronto on a filthy, slushy, gray, windy day shortly after my father died. I always experience an element of culture shock when I find myself driving in Toronto. I had moved in 1967 to a small town in eastern

Quebec, where we have one main street and one traffic light. Parking is never a problem. But in Toronto, before you can accomplish anything you have to find a parking place. After locating the downtown office I made my way down Bay Street, and left the car in an exorbitantly priced parking lot.

I breezed up the stairs of the Community and Social Services offices. As soon as I had the necessary document I was going to slip over to the Children's Aid office on Charles Street and fill in the application for my non-identifying information.

I had a lot to learn.

Filling the tiny records office was a desk dominated by a large harridan. When my turn came I asked for a copy of my adoption order. I can hear her now, as she demanded, "What do you want that for?" I was completely taken aback. This was a records office, after all, and she was a public servant. I was simply requesting a document, to which I had a right. It was *my* adoption order! It was another indication to me that I was doing something questionable, suspect, if not wrong.

"I need it for my records," I replied.

Perhaps she was tired of looking up files, perhaps she had an adopted son or daughter or niece or nephew, and had a personal axe to grind. Whatever her excuse, sympathy with my situation was not within her frame of reference. She glowered at me over her glasses and curtly informed me that I wouldn't find anything helpful in it. All I could think was that if there wasn't anything helpful contained in it, why was she being so abrasive? She was Scylla and Charybdis rolled into one, the personification of all the discriminatory laws, all the antiquated attitudes towards open records. This was not what I needed at the very beginning of my search.

On the other hand, her attitude hardened me by presenting me with a clear and typical example of what I was up against. I consciously controlled myself, for I can and do lose my temper very quickly when I encounter obvious stonewalling, and the temptation to give vent to my feelings was strong. I smiled politely and told her that it really didn't matter if it was a blank page, but that I would like to have it. I passed over my five dollars, signed a paper, and was grudgingly told that the document would be mailed to me in the fullness of time. I slipped out of the office feeling I had somehow done something dirty and immoral.

I was still innocent about official attitudes and reactions to requests for information. I am a very straightforward person and it took me some time to accept that it *is* necessary to lie. Well, perhaps not *exactly* lie, but certainly to phrase things in such a way that the listener or reader can interpret what you are saying in a light acceptable to his frame of reference. A "cover story," justifying your request, is an absolute necessity. The standard one is that you are doing family research, or genealogical research. This, of course, is not a lie at all — but you must take great care not to let slip that it is a "first family" you are interested in and that you are a searching adoptee. If the official you are dealing with suspects the truth, your request, even for the most innocuous piece of information, is doomed.

The adoption laws still in force in Ontario in the early 1980s had been made in a time when the world was very different, and their intent seems to have been solely to

protect the adults involved. Adopting couples were assured that the records would remain sealed and that their
child (as she was now) would never have access to them.
It was their choice whether this child would ever know
the facts of her true heritage. Many adopted persons may
never have known that they were not their parents'
natural offspring. Birth mothers were assured that their
past was behind them, and could safely be forgotten.
This, indeed, is the core of the problem regarding open
records. A society had given its word, backed up by
legislation, that these secrets would be guarded *for all
time.* Unfortunately, the implications for all parties had
not been given equal consideration. Is there not a point
at which the desire of the adult adoptee to know his
origin outweighs the parents' wish for secrecy? At what
point is it right to admit that certain assumptions, such
as the necessity of secrecy, were made a lifetime ago, and
may no longer be valid? As one writer has put it:

> The British National Council for Civil Liberties says
> that a child's new parents would be required by the
> court legalizing the adoption to tell the child that he
> is adopted. Their report, "Children Have Rights,"
> states: "This not only puts the relationship between
> parents and child on an honest basis but indicates
> the parents are being honest with themselves about
> the fact the child is adopted."
> Betty Reid Marshall, *Where Are the Children*

At the time that I began my search a frustrated adoptee
had nowhere to turn for help. Social workers and bureau-
crats were guardians of the law. There was no one to

persuade, there was no appeal court, no committee, nothing! This is now changing in most jurisdictions in Canada, but at that time there was no option but to find ways past and around the laws by fair means or foul. Even now the records remain sealed and unless one finds one's birth parents through mutual registration in the Adoption Disclosure Registry (see Appendix IV), there is absolutely no way that an adoptee can find out the truth, except by a personal search.

Weeks passed while I waited for my adoption order to arrive. Having no idea how long it took to receive forms, I watched the mail like a hawk for some time. Then, losing hope, I almost forgot about my request. It wasn't until December, nine months later, that a large brown envelope appeared, wrapped up with all the magazines and general advertising. I often get such envelopes in the course of business and didn't even glance at the return address. Expecting another advertising flyer I whipped out the official-looking papers. "Province of Ontario" . . . my eyes ran farther down the page . . . ALLEYNE PATRICIA ATTWOOD. It was my adoption order.

What a shock, to read that name, and a second later realize that it was my own, my birth name. The bottom half of the document confirmed the fact of my adoption and recorded the name change.

I sat stunned, staring at my middle name while memories of a long-forgotten schoolyard conversation with teenage friends came flooding back. We had been talking about our names and why our parents had chosen them for us. There were a number of Barbara Anns and Marilyns in my day, named after Barbara Ann Scott, the skater, and Marilyn Bell, the swimmer. My friends re-

counted these and the other usual reasons — they were
named for great-aunts, or their mothers had been reading a novel and liked the name of the heroine. I always
believed that the significance of given names should
come from their place in family history. Madelene was
my adoptive mother's closest childhood friend, and although I don't particularly like the name, it is important
to me and I still feel a special connection with the lovely
elderly lady whose name I bear. Unfortunately, as a child
I was slightly embarrassed about my name because it
was so different. Not until I came to Quebec did I ever
meet another Madelene outside the family.

Now, looking at the words Alleyne Patricia Attwood,
I vividly remembered that recess conversation. My
friends asked what name I would have chosen for myself. Without even thinking, I said, "Pat." Coincidence?
But there it was in black and white — I really was a Pat!

Alleyne Patricia — this was the touchstone with my
genealogical family. Who was Alleyne? Who was Patricia? Who had given me this name? What was she like?
Why did she choose those particular names out of all the
hundreds of names available? I was instantly sure that
the person who named me Pat must be a good type. Silly,
perhaps, but those are the thoughts that ran through my
mind. (I was to discover later that Patricia was a very
special friend of my birth father's and the name by which
he and my birth mother had always remembered me.)

The letter enclosed with the adoption order simply
said: "We have received the sworn affidavit in support
of an application for a copy of your adoption order. A
certified copy of the order is enclosed as requested." Was
that what I had signed? I am still mystified by how easy

it was to obtain this one document, for it certainly falls under the category of identifying information. I later learned that it was only before 1970 that the birth name of the child appeared on the document. After that date, unless the judge, the court or the adoptive parents decided for a specific reason that the full birth name should appear, only the initial of the birth surname would appear. Today, this document is only available to adoptees who know their original surname, because it would be a source of identifying information if this was not the case. There was a window of only a few months when one could apply and receive the adoption order without knowing the birth name. I was certainly fortunate. Without it and the disclosure of my birth name, I never would have been able to even start my search.

Now I had a name to work with. But whose name was it? My birth mother's? My birth father's? In the normal course of events a child born to an unmarried mother takes the name of the mother. Unmarried? I didn't know. But why else would I have been put up for adoption?

A name can be traced, and I was determined to track down this unknown male or female Attwood. If it was my mother's name, it would be a great deal more difficult to find her, because she was likely to have married and changed her name. However, I would persevere! Thankfully, my original surname was an unusual one. Had it been Smith or Jones, or any one of a score of surnames, it would have been a much more difficult, perhaps even an impossible, quest.

I now had two vital pieces of information: I was born Alleyne Patricia Attwood, in the town of Barrie, Ontario. I soon found that it was unwise to simply shoot from the hip as ideas for information sources occur. You must have a plan. Institutions have definite policies and procedures for giving out information. For valid reasons much of this should not be handed out to just anyone who comes by.

A search is carried out by imagining possibilities and then eliminating them, one by one, until, as in a Euclidean geometry problem, the only thing left is the correct answer. The first step was to discover whether my adoption had been done privately or through a Children's Aid Society. The easiest to eliminate would be an agency adoption.

I wrote to Children's Aid in Barrie in November of 1982. A mere two weeks later a letter arrived from a social worker:

I have attempted to locate information regarding your adoption in our Agency's records. Unfortunately, based upon the data you have provided this effort has been unsuccessful. Perhaps your adoption was arranged privately and if so, we would not have a record of this.

If your adoption took place through a Children's Aid Society it would not have been finalized for at least six months. [In actual fact, the time period in 1942 was two years — M.A.] Do you have a copy of the adoption order? This would list in what court the adoption was finalized and also in those years the natural name of the child was usually listed on the adoption order. If we knew your natural mother's name we could check and see if we have any record of her.

Perhaps you were placed by another Children's Aid Society. Oftentimes mothers had their babies placed in Toronto and that agency handled the adoption. You might contact either of the two agencies in that city regarding this possibility.

I am sorry that without more information we cannot be more helpful or specific. If you learn of any different or new details please contact us.

In my eagerness to gain information, I had not thought to send my birth name! I decided to write to the Children's Aid Society of Metropolitan Toronto before writing back to Barrie and received the following reply shortly afterward:

We have received your inquiry requesting non-identifying information. We have checked our records to confirm that there is information available. However, because we are receiving an INCREASING NUMBER of requests such as yours, we have had to establish a waiting list. It will be approximately 18 months before your files can be studied and the information prepared for you. Do be assured that we will give your request attention as soon as possible.

I now took my place in the queue, but this in itself was reassuring, inasmuch as it was a confirmation that there were many people who wanted the same thing and who had embarked on the same quest. However, unlike a bank line-up, where no matter how slowly you move forward you can see the line getting shorter, there is no sense of progress in this category of waiting. Eighteen months seemed an impossibly long time.

I began to assimilate the vocabulary of adoption. Even government and social workers used a variety of terms to refer to the various individuals involved in the adoption triangle. This terminology is often confusing, especially the terms for parents. The social worker from Barrie referred to my natural parents, other letters referred to my birth parents. Non-professionals tend to refer to these shadowy figures as *real* parents.

The question of the *real* versus the *not real* is interesting. Margery Williams deals with it in her charming children's book, *The Velveteen Rabbit*, which tells the story of a stuffed toy rabbit that is given to a child. After the nursery lights are out the rabbit makes friends with a ragged old stuffed horse. One day he asks the horse, "What is real?" and is told, "Real isn't how you are made, it is a thing that happens to you. When a child loves you for a long, long time, not just to play with, but REALLY loves you, then you become Real." The rabbit persists, "Does it happen all at once, like being wound up, or just bit by bit?" "It doesn't happen all at once," comes the answer. "You become. It takes a long time."

Our adoptive parents have become real to us through the love that has grown over the years. Our birth parents, because we do not know them except as murky figures in our history, are not real to us. It is only through the discovery of our past that we in turn become real *to ourselves*. We do not become less through knowledge; we become fulfilled and whole.

The magic of love acts on the rabbit, and he finally hops off to play with the real rabbits whom he had only been able to sit and watch from a distance. We have imagined one family and grown up in another, but family ties with both families become complete only when reality touches us in its fullness. The people we have known and loved for "a long, long time" are our adoptive parents. If we use this definition, then they are our real parents.

We also hear the term "natural" parents used in reference to our birth parents, and thus, following logical grammatical rules of opposites, this must mean that our adoptive parents are unnatural. Not many adoptive parents would be in favour of this terminology!

"Birth" or "biological" parents are cold terms that ignore the possibility that one or both of these people loved the child, and remembered him after he was given up. All these terms imply a value judgement: that one kind of parent is better than the other. One family has their *own* children, their neighbours have an *adopted* child. These terms are in such general use by legislators and social workers, as well as the friends and family of those affected by adoption, that the implications are glossed over. The terms have no deeper meaning (or power to hurt) except to those who are specifically touched by them, be they adoptive parents, birth parents or the children. Even they have become immune to the painful implications of words in such common use.

I still find all these terms cold and clinical, even offensive. Allow me to offer the following terms and definitions. My adoptive parents were my psychological parents. They gave me my nurturing and my philosophy of life, an environment, and a background for my growing up. My birth parents were those through whose love for each other I was given life and that very special combination of genes that binds me forever to my original family tree. I was grafted on to, not assimilated by, another family.

By this time, in 1982, I had joined Parent Finders and found their regular newsletter not only helpful but also encouraging. Included with the newsletter was information about the Voluntary Disclosure Registry of the Ontario Government, which was created in 1978 in a restructuring of the Child Welfare Act that enabled adult adoptees and birth parents to meet or exchange information. This was a passive registry — both parties must register for there to be any possibility of contact — in contrast to an active registry, where employees will actively search for the missing party. With the passive registry, I like to think that bells ring and lights flash if the computer comes up with a match. (I am sure, however, that it is much more mundane. But surely there is at least a "Hey George, I got one!" and a slight smile of triumph from the employee.) If a match is made, each party is contacted and arrangements are made for counselling and possible reunion.

The registry is a marvellous idea, but only to a point, because its existence is not widely publicized. Birth parents were never directly contacted when the service began, so unless someone was actively searching knowledgeably about current literature on the topic, or was a member of a group such as Parent Finders, he or she would probably never learn about the registry's existence.

Human rights have taken a quantum leap forward in the last decade, so far as family relationships and the rights of children are concerned. For example, children over twelve have the right to be involved in custody negotiations when their parents divorce, and teenagers may get medical treatment for a wide range of illnesses and conditions without parental knowledge. However, at the time of my search, the rules governing the Voluntary Disclosure Registry (now known as the Adoption Disclosure Registry) stated that the permission of the adoptive parents must be given before any steps could be taken for contacting the birth parents. This put a real crimp in the system, and rendered it almost useless; it created situations where two consenting, related adults wished to meet, but the permission of a third party, with a very different set of priorities and worries, had to be obtained first. Whether the adoptee is eighteen or fifty, she must turn to her adoptive parents and say, "Please, may I have your permission?"

Not only was this a blatant infringement of human rights but it was a cruel and unreasonable requirement. Under no other circumstances do parents have such rights over their adult "offspring." Thankfully, this draconian regulation was removed from the passage in the Act of 1987. Before that change, it was possible that an adoptee might find himself in a situation where elderly, infirm parents are incapable of making a decision of such magnitude. I simply could not imagine myself thrusting a piece of paper into my father's frail hands as he lay in a hospital, which he would never leave, and saying: "By the way, Dad, I'm looking for my birth parents and have found them on the registry. Would you be good enough to sign this so I can meet them?" In these cases the adoptee simply did not meet the birth parents through legal or official channels.

Had a match been made, indicating that my birth mother was also searching for me, I would not have been able to meet her, and the frustration would have been pure torture. This scenario never became fact in my case, but may well have.

How many elderly adoptive parents would willingly give their child permission to go through with a contact with their birth parents should the registry come up with a match? Much as one would like to think of adoption as an open topic in families, in many, especially of our middle-aged generation, it is not.

3

THE NEED
TO SEARCH

For some applicants the activity of seeking
information became satisfying for its own
sake and they found that the more
information they obtained, the more they
wanted. They enjoyed the search and became
more intrigued concerning the person about
whom they were collecting information.

Erica Haimes and Noel Timms,
Adoption, Identity, and Social Policy

E VERY SEARCHING ADOPTEE at some point must face the
frustration of sealed records, the foundation of the
adoption game. There has "been an assumption that
adoptees and birth parents would never need to know
each other, that adoptees would never ask why they were
surrendered, and that birth parents would not be concerned about their child's subsequent development"
(Silverman et al., *Reunions between Adoptees and Birth
Parents*).

The rules of the game are quite simple and I learned
them early on. Be happy with the status quo. Do not rock

the boat. Any information must be given by adoptive parents. Nobody gave me a handbook and certainly nobody told me that the corollary to these rules was that if my adoptive parents did not wish to reveal any details of my background then I must be satisfied, accept the situation as it was and play the game with good grace. *I just knew.*

Games are an important part of our society. We play games with our children to teach them good sportsmanship, the grace of winning and the importance of being a good loser. As adults many of us follow professional sport or take part in team sports. We belong to bridge clubs, or enjoy the odd game of Trivial Pursuit with friends. Games are synonymous with relaxation and companionship. As a camp director I am always on the lookout for new games. I haunt bookstores, waiting for new volumes. I accidentally came across a most thought-provoking volume erroneously filed under games. A bookstore clerk had simply gone by the title, *Finite and Infinite Games*, and had not bothered to look at the contents before shelving it. This little book by James Carse was not full of ingenious games but dealt with the philosophy of play in the framework of life itself. One concept struck me as particularly poignant when related to the life of an adoptee:

> A finite game is played for the purpose of winning, an infinite game for the purpose of continuing the play. It may appear that the approval of the spectators, or the referees, is also required in the determination of the winner. . . . Suppose the players all agree, but the spectators and the referees do not.

Unless the players can be persuaded that their agreement was mistaken, they will not resume the play — indeed they cannot resume the play.

This seemed to put the adoption game into perspective, to shift it away from the perspective of a simple "us against them" adversarial situation and to give its implications a far broader perspective. The game, as I was defining it, was a finite game. I wanted to win. If the rules were not going to be rewritten by the referees, then I was going to write my own rules and join others in demanding that the rules be rewritten according to our definition of what the game should reflect. We were demanding rules that would turn their infinite game into a finite one, a game with a beginning and an end, as contrasted to the lawmakers' concept of an endless game. To be involved in the adoption game is to be bound into a world within a world. It is a contest which has its own teams, rules, cheering section, winners, losers and referees. Life is the field on which it is played. The finite end of the adoption game is knowledge. The infinite game simply means adoptees go through their whole lives without the right to know.

The same society that has taken such giant strides in the areas of divorce reform, abortion reform, the acceptance of homosexuality and a myriad other far-reaching reforms has only taken minute and long-delayed steps to recognize that adoptees have any legal right to know their past. The recognition that we have a right to a life complete with the knowledge of our heritage, culture and medical history is slow in coming. The rules have been changing during the past decade simply because a growing number of dedicated people within the community, both players (adoptees, some birth families and some adoptive families), and referees (enlightened social workers and legislators) are redefining their definitions of who should be the winners. The referees are still not sure how to cope with our two sets of parents and their rights and concerns. They become confused when they realize that many birth and adoptive parents also want the rules changed. The turmoil over release of information — how it is to be done, how much to give, and when — will reign until there is agreement as to what kind of game we all are playing. Other questions must also be answered, such as who is protecting whom, and why and at what cost. Unfortunately, some spectators are still in doubt about the validity and seriousness of the game, and some referees don't want it played at all.

My attitude to my status changed during this period of waiting. Instead of being ashamed of admitting that I was searching, I began to speak about it to friends and colleagues. At first I was met with the attitude of "That's interesting, and what did you do last weekend?" After a time that changed, as they learned more and realized the depth of my frustration. Many expressed surprise at the archaic attitude of the law in relation to adoptees. They had never realized that adoptees are different from others in the eyes of the law. They were amazed to hear that adoptees can only receive a short-form birth certificate, which does not contain the names of our birth parents, and horrified that not only is our original birth certificate not available to us, but since the 1960s adoptive parents have been required to complete and sign an amended "statement of live birth," substituting their names and other information for the original names.

The non-adopted take their medical history for granted. No adoptee ever does, for our medical history is not available unless our life is threatened. Even if the documents are released (to the doctors only) there may be nothing in our records. No procedure was ever built into the adoption process to collect information about our ageing parents or grandparents. Our adoptive parents were only given a very rough outline of the health of our birth parents, and (except in rare cases) no family medical history was recorded. To get medical information about our birth family now entails a court order for the opening of birth records. Despite requests from the medical profession, it is the lawyers who make the final judgement on whether this information is necessary.

I did not become calmer after I had made the decision to search; in fact, my anger grew. I felt an unreasonable resentment every time an article appeared in the paper about prejudice or human rights. Not that I begrudged any minority groups their valid rights, but my inner voice screamed, "What about us?" In a heated discussion with a friend I said that nobody really cares about the adoptee as a separate entity. The average person hears about adoption only as it may affect their family or friends, or as a passing reference in a newspaper article or notice. They may read that "A and B are happy to announce the arrival of their *chosen* child." I asked her how often she had considered this announcement further — had she ever thought about the difference between choice and birth? What are they going to do with it now that they have chosen it?

Upon what do you base a choice? Race? Family background, if it is known? Dimpled cheeks? Uncle Harry's
nose? There is no refund if not completely satisfied. A
family chooses a house, a car, a dog. In that sense, the
child may become a possession in the sense that a conceived child is not. I tried to explain the difference with
the example of my own children. I have never felt that I
possess my children; they were given to us. We conceived them and we did our best to bring them up. One
day they existed in my womb, although the day before
that they had not; it is as simple as that. But parents who
adopt make a deliberate choice, on a particular day, to
set in motion the process that will bring a child born of
others into their lives. There is a deliberateness, which is
not the same as with a couple who are hoping to conceive
a child. It is certain that this attitude must affect the way
the adoptive parents see and treat and bring up their
child.

A friend, who has four adopted children, told me that
some time before they expected a new addition to the
family, they were telephoned from the city and told that
their child was ready to be picked up!

One reads of the shortage of adoptable children and of
the number of adults who are desperate to find a child.
This puts us as a commodity on the market — there is a
shortage of oil, therefore it must be imported — there is
a shortage of endemic Canadian children, so there is a
need to import children from other lands.

Things were very different in the first half of the twentieth century when there was no dearth of unwanted
Canadian children, and I will never deny that those of us
who entered the world on the wrong side of the blanket,

or who were born into deprived families, are grateful for the chance of a "better" life. We are different, but this does not change our rights to knowledge of our background.

In my reading I came across the term "psychological vagrant" in reference to adoptees who wish to know their roots. The word "vagrant" shocked me more than any other description I have heard. How could anyone be so cruel as to apply such a phrase, with its connotations of aimlessness and beggary, to individuals who simply want to place themselves in a genealogical framework?

A search cannot be constant. I discovered quickly that no matter how much I wanted to focus all my time and energy on it the other aspects of my life did not come to a halt. I had my family and a business. A search is time-consuming; it requires not only letter-writing, telephone calls and reading, but also intensive contemplation and re-evaluation of motives in preparation for the final outcome. Emotionally you soar to heights of excitement and hope, then plunge to depths of despair as a vitally important lead turns out to be useless. As the frustration grew, I sometimes wondered if it was really worth the effort.

A search tends to be on-again, off-again. You can only take so many dead ends before you find yourself cooling off. One day you just realize that you have not written that letter that you should have sent off last week, or you find yourself starting to bake again, or taking the dog for longer walks, or playing in a weekend curling bonspiel instead of concentrating intensely — as you had been doing for weeks — on the search. Then something starts

you off again, and you go back into hibernation, shun-
ning all outside interests, until you reach the next set of
dead ends. I wonder if I could have coped with the
intensity of emotions for the years my search took if I had
not paused from time to time and let other things take
precedence.

A search becomes compulsive during the "on" periods
and affects family life profoundly: invitations not accepted, evenings not shared, dinner table conversations
usurped. You announce each tiny victory, moan over
each dead end. You analyse, you repeat, you think out
loud. Fortunately, my husband was patient, nodding
sagely during my ramblings, accepting late meals on the
days when I was on a hot trail, and not complaining
about the telephone bill (which became horrendous as
my patience ebbed and I would phone instead of writing). It was more difficult for our children, who were
twelve and thirteen at the time. They simply could not
understand my obsession with finding these "other people." They had known and loved my adoptive parents
who had been Grampa and Nana to them; they missed
them, and didn't want any others.

During the long winter months from January to March,
1983, I read, studied and touched base with other adoptees, seeking to learn everything that had been "discovered" about "us." *Books in Print* directed me to all the
books available that had anything to do with adoption.
I read voraciously: sociological texts, psychology magazines, books by adoptees, books for adoptees. No one
library has a comprehensive collection on the subject.
One might think that the schools of social work at major

universities would have collections, for surely there must be some young people specializing in counselling this part of society. But no, the books came in dribs and drabs, one from this university, one from that — one from as far away as the public library in Whitehorse, Alaska.

I was looking for clues about how to find the information society said we weren't supposed to have. Had someone uncovered a loophole that would open doors? Each story involved a different set of circumstances, but through reading I acquired a range of techniques and suggestions about the type of information that could be gleaned from many different and varied sources. Books, for me, took the place of the counselling that is now mandatory in Ontario, both at the time of receipt of the non-identifying information and later, when reunion is being considered.

Sociological texts developed for me the concept that adopted children are not and cannot ever truly be "as if born" to their families. My feelings and emotions were not unusual or abnormal, but were held in common with other adoptees and had been expressed repeatedly to researchers. This, in itself, was vitally important, for I went through a period of feeling cut adrift from all that had gone before. I was afraid I might cut myself off from those whom I had previously considered family. I felt that there was no one, other than my own husband and children, to turn to. I had a perfectly good adoptive family — what ever did I think I was doing going off into the unknown?

I viewed everyone involved with the possession of my personal information in an adversarial light — the Ontario government, the Children's Aid Society and any other organization that might be sitting on files related to my family. *They* had the information and *they* were doing everything in their power to keep me from getting it!

A business trip in February, 1983, took me to western Ontario. I looked forward to dinner with a middle-aged cousin of my mother's in Guelph and then an overnight stay in Waterloo with an old camp friend. My cousin and I had a most enjoyable dinner, during which I caught up with all the family news and views. We moved with our coffee to the living room. Conversation ebbed and flowed. Suddenly, for some inexplicable reason, the topic of adoption came up. This in itself was strange, for it was never mentioned in our family. I don't remember ever having spoken of it to any of the relatives over the years. Even in the middle of my search, I had decided not to speak about it to members of the family: that would be a last resort. In any case, something led me to comment irreverently that I figured I must be the product of a "roll in the hay" between a soldier and a local girl.

I will never forget the look that crossed Mary's face. "You don't really believe that, do you?" she said in a hushed, shocked voice.

"What else can I believe?"

There was a long silence. She looked at her husband and he nodded. The silence stretched uncomfortably. "I didn't know that you didn't know."

A knot was growing in my chest. "Know what?" I whispered.

She paused, deliberately set down her coffee cup, and said, "Your parents married after the war and there were other children."

How does one react to such news? What does one say? This was something that I had never imagined. This was the first real fact I had ever heard about my birth parents. Information that my cousin thought I knew. I had been overlooking the most obvious source of information — my adoptive family.

For someone who had been brought up as an only child, but who was happiest when living with others at camp, at school, in university residence; for someone for whom friendships were the most precious thing in the world, the fact that I had full brothers and/or sisters was earth-shattering.

It was now about eight o'clock in the evening, when normally I would be saying my farewells. The friend I was staying with, whom I hadn't seen for some months, was expecting me at any time and there was a half-hour of icy roads to navigate between Guelph and Waterloo. But I couldn't leave now! While Mary put on another pot of coffee I phoned Ann, somewhat self-consciously, for it is not normal behaviour for an overnight guest to phone and say, "Something has come up, I'll be in late, don't wait up for me." I wanted to tell this special friend what was happening, what I had learned, but I couldn't bring myself to tell her on the phone. She told me later that it was a difficult time for her, wondering what had happened, and it was even more difficult when indeed she had to go to bed, knowing that I would be in "some time."

The next four hours were full of discovery, questioning, thinking and exchanging ideas. I grilled my poor cousin and her husband with the intensity of an interrogator in the Spanish Inquisition. I wanted any and every clue to the identity of my parents. Think, think! When? Where? What were you doing when . . . ? How do you know? But we were looking back forty years; it was her much older cousin who had adopted the child and she had certainly not stored up facts to reveal to me later.

Mary had entered nursing in Toronto in the late 1940s and had spent a great deal of time with my adoptive parents. She remembered vividly my mother reading a birth announcement in the paper and exclaiming, "Madelene's parents have another child." The implications were twofold: not only did I have at least one brother or sister, but my mother *knew* the identity of my birth parents and that they were married.

Here, however, were two other crucial facts. If I could determine the approximate time of year of this birth announcement, I could start searching newspapers. If Attwood was indeed my father's name, the announcement would give me first names. If Attwood was my mother's, the process would be longer, but the outcome should be the same. (I was not to know until later that including the mother's maiden name in birth announcements was not a common practice at that time.)

Pinpointing the time was not as simple as I expected. "Were you just starting training?" I asked my cousin. "Was it near exams? Was it summer, winter?" Perhaps she was one of these people who remembered settings, who would get flashbacks of minor details of a room. "Can you remember what you were wearing? Was the window open?" *Any* clue as to the season? But she couldn't remember. Generalities, yes, but not specifics — nothing that would give me something to go on.

We dredged the past, into the subconscious. One small

detail led to another. By this time I was taking notes, terrified that in the emotion of the night I would forget some tiny, crucial detail. My birth father had been an army officer. The family had moved out west. Vital clues. How did she know these things? By listening to the same veranda conversations with the old aunts as I had. I had been too young, I had only picked up the vibes of mystery, but she had known the connection and was twenty years older than I was. She remembered the undercurrents, and thought she had heard that I had spent two weeks with my parents before I was given up.

I treasure the letter that Mary sent me shortly after my visit:

> All that information seemed to come from the depths of my subconscious. I just could not in good conscience let you think what you thought. . . . You asked, I gave . . . all very fascinating. For your own mental well-being you could dismiss it all as "hearsay" from a cousin in the senility nursery. Keep in touch and ask anything you may think of. P.S. Deep down feeling that something good will happen.

That evening, I finally tore myself away and headed down the dark, icy midnight road. My mind drifted dangerously more than once. I was exhausted, emotionally and physically. It was a familiar route, for I had driven it many times in daylight between the universities of Guelph and Waterloo, but it had never stretched so bleakly before.

At last the familiar turn-off loomed out of the darkness. Sinnders, my friend's schnauzer, was determined to give me his usual royal welcome when at last I slipped in the door, briefcase in one hand, suitcase in the other. He was a bounding bundle of gray, yipping fluff trying to reach my face for a wet kiss. One half of me tried to keep him quiet as I knelt down for the expected cuddle, the other half prayed that these excited yips *would* wake his mistress. I needed to talk.

It was by now well past one in the morning and the friendly barks had done their work. Bleary-eyed, Ann appeared at the head of the stairs. She rushed down and held me in a long sisterly hug. We sat down at the kitchen table, but I couldn't stay still. I was shaking as I began to tell her what had happened in Guelph. The very stiff drink she poured me was most welcome. I jumped from one thing to another, and the words came pouring out. As I told Ann what had happened, the actual act of verbalizing what Mary had told me made the impact, and the import, even greater. (As this dear friend wrote to me later: "I knew that you were really shaken because your freckles had disappeared!")

I had only once mentioned to her, many years before, that I was adopted, and I had never mentioned my project. She had known my adoptive family and had been a frequent guest in our home. Friends had been very important to me before my search, but as it progressed, their warmth and love and interest took on a whole new dimension. Two hours later, only four hours before she had to get up to face a class of eager students, we separated to get some sleep at last. (She told me later that she had been so moved by the experience that she told her students the next morning about her friend's quest, and throughout the rest of my search, her school children excitedly waited for each new installment.)

It is impossible to describe the feeling one has when one's whole sense of self is changed. I was exhausted, but exhilarated. Before I slept, I found a scrap of paper, and wrote this:

> The most incredible thing has happened! I have brothers and sisters, or at least siblings. I can't believe it! My whole world has turned completely around. After forty years there are people of my own flesh and blood — it's almost too much to comprehend. I simply didn't know how to even view it. One thing I do know, I must find them. I know I must realize that they, perhaps, couldn't care less — they have a family unit with an eldest and a youngest — that there is another "eldest" may not even be within their frame of reference. Who are those unnamed they? Is one by chance the girl on the train? [In 1974 I had seen a girl on the train from Toronto to Montreal who bore a striking resemblance to me. We kept meeting each other's eye, but we never spoke.] WHO ARE THEY? I don't even know their surname for sure. The consciousness of birth parents is no longer number one — it is their other children — FULL brothers and/or sisters. WHO ARE THEY?

There was no time to chat in the morning as Ann went off to school, but later she wrote me: "The next morning, I had all the energy of a run-over chicken, and you looked fresh-faced and bright-eyed like a flower out to nab a bee or two." I don't remember being quite so wide awake, but do remember feeling a fundamental happiness greater than any I had ever known.

For the next three years I would have an additional reason for going to Ontario. I found that some of my most productive reflection and reasoning was done on the road, away from the demands of home. The long route down the 401 and the Eastern Townships Autoroute between Lennoxville and Toronto was so familiar that the car almost drove itself while I went up and down metaphorical roads of contemplation. I learned to keep a tape recorder on the passenger seat to capture thoughts and ideas and to make note of side roads that looked worth travelling.

Some of my most fruitful evaluation and deliberation was done in the lounge of the Fireside Inn in Kingston, my half-way spot. I have been staying here for well over fifteen years and it feels like home away from home. When I check in, there is always time for a welcome chat with staff, who have become friends. The lounge, with its congenial atmosphere, deep chairs, glowing fire, coupled with quiet music and conversation, provided an oasis where I could ponder the revelations of the last hectic few days.

It was here, two nights after the great discovery, that I wrote the most difficult letters of my life. Mary had known so much. What did others know? The time had come to face my fears of guilt and rejection and to ask family and friends for information. Encouraged by the outpouring of understanding from Mary, I felt bold enough to approach those who had been closest to my parents.

I wrote three letters that night, one to my namesake and the others to my mother's most intimate friends. I tried to explain as clearly as possible what had happened, what I had discovered, how I felt and why I wanted to search. I wrote of my feelings towards my adoptive family, of my love for them and of my understanding of how important I had been to them. I tried to express my loyalty to my family and to the memory of my parents. I begged for understanding and assistance.

Self-image is so important. I had always been seen by these people as the "special" daughter. However, I was terrified that they would see me now as ungrateful and unloving, or that they would think I was trying to find a replacement family now that my parents were dead. I lay awake until the small hours worrying about the reaction of these people who knew me so well as the loving daughter of their dearest friends. Had I done the right thing? Would I lose the support of people who had been important to me in my growing-up years and who still held a special place in my life? I really was afraid. I had lived for the past twenty years in another province, and it was only this slender thread that held me to all that I had known in my childhood.

With fearful heart I dropped the envelopes in the mail the next morning. I had confessed my innermost needs to those who would be most likely to condemn me. I could only wait, praying that they would understand and even be able to tell me, if not the whole story, then bits or pieces that would expand my knowledge.

My first goal was to establish my birth mother's name. Since she had eventually married my father there was always the chance that he had given me his name. I pushed to the back of my mind what I would do if my queries led me first to one of my siblings. The last thing I wanted to do was barge into the lives of these unknown siblings, who probably did not even know of my existence. It would be the rare mother who would tell her children of a child born before her marriage.

When I reached home, I telephoned my eldest cousin on my father's side. She was surprised at my news, but reacted positively to my questions. Why had I assumed that people would be against me? She, too, remembered general things and now I can't remember what facts came at what stage for we had many long-distance conversations. She told me that my father had been in the military, in the insurance business and a member of a lodge. Her father, my uncle, had been a lawyer; his firm had handled the adoption. It really had been "all in the family" — the doctor who delivered me had been a classmate of my father's (he was also, as I was to discover later, my birth mother's family doctor, and had been sworn to secrecy). I don't understand why they didn't just do the whole thing privately without getting the Children's Aid involved! But thank heavens they did.

When I learned of my uncle's involvement, I immediately thought that his papers might still be in existence, for they would be outside the jurisdiction of sealed records. But disappointment followed fast on the heels of anticipation. In the next breath she told me that his papers were long gone, as he had been dead almost twenty years. She went on to say that she thought that my birth father had been a patient in the T.B. sanitorium in Gravenhurst. (This was a classic case of mixed information. As it turned out it was my mother who had been connected with "the San," for she worked there as a dietitian.) This was interesting because my adoptive father had been with the Department of Veterans' Affairs and had regularly examined patients at the sanatorium. I remembered having to wait in the car when we stopped for one of his appointments on the way to our cottage in Muskoka. Maybe my parents had been afraid that my birth father would appear. (When I told my birth mother about this some time later, her comment was, "Perhaps I was playing on the lawn with your brother.")

My cousin thought that my birth father must have died some time in the 1960s while my adoptive father was still working with the D.V.A.; she remembered that he told her that he had seen my birth father's pension file. Therefore he must have died before my adoptive father retired in the fall of 1964. (I was later to learn that he died on St. Valentine's day of that year.)

An individual was now taking shape, but he was still a phantom whom I would never meet. And still he had no name.

It is interesting the tiny things people remember. My cousin recalled the name Bainbridge; it rang a bell in the depths of her subconscious — or maybe it was just a short name starting with B. These hints, often contradictory, are enough to drive you mad.

The responses to my letters began to arrive one after another in close succession. Though I thought that my mother might have confided in her, my namesake wrote a loving, supportive letter — but she knew nothing apart from the fact that I was adopted. Her concluding sentence was so compelling: "I think you should consider your search daily — you would feel so much more satisfied."

Another letter concluded, "It is so understandable, what you are trying to find out about your birth parents. . . . There is no reason if you met it should not be a happy reunion."

Why had I been so enveloped in fear? The legacy of secrecy is poisonous, and it had permeated my being far more deeply than I knew; I only realized how deeply when I finally came to grips with the anxiety of my preconceived guilt. Some of that guilt ebbed away with the receipt of these letters, but still I constantly needed reassurance that I was not being disloyal. If my adoptive parents had had any inkling of the repercussions of their actions and attitudes, they might have reacted differently to the counsel of secrecy. I struggled for a long time with the basic inconsistency of their legacy to me: on the one hand scrupulous honesty, on the other deliberate evasion of the truth.

To discover if Attwood was my mother's or father's name I decided to write for my records from the Barrie hospital. This seemed innocuous enough, for I had seen my own children's charts, and my name had been on them; surely this would be open information. I wrote to the Royal Victoria Hospital under the name of Alleyne Attwood — not really an untruth, for I had been A. Attwood at the time the report had been made. If I had written using my present name, I certainly would not have obtained the information, any more than I could have had access to the records of Joe Blow. I simply explained that I needed my birth records for medical reasons. Perhaps it would have been better to have asked my friendly family doctor to write on my behalf, for I soon received the following reply: "In reference to your recent letter, enclosed is a copy of the Temperature and Weight chart, which is the only birth information which is on record for yourself. We trust this will be of assistance to you." And there, on obviously yellowed graph paper, were two wavy lines between July 3 and July 17, 1942, labelled "Baby Attwood, Ward — Nursery." I held in my hand this chart, history number 1011, recording the birth of an infant who had weighed into this world at seven pounds, seven ounces, one July day forty-one years before. All it told me was that I had been discharged at 6:15 p.m. thirteen days later by a Mrs. Whiteside. Discharged where, and with whom? Somehow I expected there would be discharge papers with my mother's name and address on them or at least some clue! To this day I honestly cannot believe that somewhere deep within the bowels of that hospital there is not a record of where this Baby Attwood came from. According to the records that I was given, I had simply materialized! A subsequent request for my mother's files was, as I had expected, denied. But now I was more certain that Attwood was my mother's name.

The order in which one asked for facts proved important. Even a few details can make a request appear legitimate. If the order of requesting information was reversed — B before A — I would be met with refusal, because I obviously didn't know something that a "normal" person would know as a matter of course. Officials seem to have antennae that alert them to requests from adoptees. If you do not have legitimate reasons to ask for information, the door will be slammed in your face. I wrote for my parents' marriage certificate, to discover if Attwood was my mother or father's name. Normally, a daughter would identify her parents by their full names — an ambiguous request sets the bells ringing. I received a form letter telling me that the signature of one of the principals was required. There was also a personal note suggesting that I contact the Adoption Disclosure Registry. I had mentioned nothing about being adopted in my original request. You can't hide it!

It is difficult to go back to the same office with the same request several weeks later, even if by then you have data that would make the original request seem legitimate. You might be lucky and meet a different person, or the original clerk might not remember, but in all likelihood your request, because it was unusual, will be remembered. This puts you in a difficult position. If a second request is denied you may wonder if it is only because they have become suspicious about your story, and there is very little you can do about that.

At each step you must analyse the information to be sure that you have gleaned all of its implications. Time must be taken to ponder where each tiny fragment of information might lead. Every fragment is a key, and one of them, eventually, will turn out to be the golden key to knowledge.

It was now the middle of the summer, 1982, and I had exhausted all my leads. I was feeling thoroughly discouraged. All I could do now was wait for the non-identifying information to come from the Children's Aid Society.

4

"NON-IDENTIFYING" INFORMATION

> *The social organization of adoptions and the*
> *assumptions of adoption practitioners and*
> *researchers actually help to create*
> *advantageous situations for the adoptee to*
> *negotiate in order to display their mental*
> *stability and thus prove their competence to*
> *handle apparently "dangerous" information.*
> Erica Haimes and Noel Timms,
> *Adoption, Identity, and Social Policy*

M Y NON-IDENTIFYING INFORMATION arrived at the beginning of February, 1984, only nine months (not
eighteen!) after my application to Children's Aid. Two simple typewritten pages. They looked so innocuous, but here,
in my hands, was my past and my future, in words which
not only put flesh on the shadowy figures of my parents,
but also began to fill in my missing genealogy.

You were born on July 3, 1942 in Barrie, Ontario, were
cared for by your birth mother for your first two weeks
of life and then in a Mothercraft home while she and

your birth father sorted out the best plan for you. . . .
Your birth mother and father shared equally in the
decision — wanted you to have a stable, secure,
loving home to grow up in and decided adoption
would be the best way to ensure this for you.

So I was not one of those children who were snatched from
their mother by well-meaning social workers! I felt no
anger, only pity for that couple who had had "to figure
out the best plan." If they had not loved me, they would
not have kept me even that long. How could something
that had happened so many years ago, at a time when I
was not even cognizant of what was going on, matter so
much? I felt a warmth that I had not known before towards
these people. A conviction that I was doing the right thing
in searching for them swept over me.

Your birth mother was 30 years old, single, born in
Ontario. She was 5′ 2½″ tall, weighed 118 pounds,
had thick dark auburn hair, high colour with some
freckles, dark expressive brown eyes, regular fea-
tures, oval-shaped face. She was poised in manner,
able to control her feelings, showed marked willingness to co-operate in planning for you.

Apart from her height, I felt that I was looking in a mirror.
But the description was so clinical! This was my mother
who was being described, not a subject in some sociological study.

Her father was 5′ 6″ tall, well-built, similar in colouring, very active and healthy. His interests were

centered in his home and family.... Her mother was
described as a good mother and homemaker, who
loved music, had an excellent voice, exposed her
family to music.

My grandparents, whom I would never meet. I wondered if they knew about me. I thought not, considering
the attitudes at the time.

I could imagine my adoptive parents reading this
information half a lifetime ago. The fact that my birth
mother had been musical ("She played the piano, sang
in the church choir") would certainly have appealed to
my adoptive mother, for she had been a pianist and had
continued to teach and accompany throughout her life.
One of her great sorrows was that no matter how long
this daughter practised, she was never going to be a
musician. The genes had let us down!

My birth mother had enjoyed sports, liked to knit and
sew, and read widely. I could not help thinking that if we
ever met we would have a great deal in common.

My heritage was British, for her parents had both
emigrated from England, as had my birth father. I had
three aunts on my mother's side. My father had been
forty-two when I was born, and had been in the army in
both world wars. His brother had died at seventeen,
cause unknown, and his mother had died from shock
after the total demolition of her house in England during
a bombing raid early in the Second World War.

These were now real people, with a real history. I had
a description of my family, albeit a somewhat vague one,
but I wanted to know if I resembled any of them in a
physical sense — other than freckles! How nice an anon-

ymous photograph would have been just to see them. However, I realized that this certainly would not be practical. How surprising it would be, if one lived in a small community, to see the youthful face of the friendly neighbourhood storekeeper or bank teller staring out at you from a yellowed photograph!

The emotions those two pages aroused are as real to me now as they were at that moment. They were akin to the feelings that enveloped me when I first saw my birth name. What I had read were details of strangers, yet they were *my parents*. When one reads a biography, one is interested in the character of the individual, and usually this curiosity is satisfied. Yet all I was given here were the most rudimentary facts, about two people who should have been closest of all to me — and I was expected to be satisfied!

I was not satisfied. These scraps of description only challenged me to go on. I had to turn these unrelated facts into the identifying information that would lead me to the people they represented. The real detective work started the moment I laid the papers back down on my desk. I scrutinized the data and stretched my imagination to the limits, weighing each fact, searching for half-hidden signs, arrows pointing onward to the next discovery. A plan of action slowly started to form. The process of observation, deduction and planning could be schematized something like this:

Fact: "Your birth father was 42 years old, unhappily married and in the Armed Services overseas." Birth date here of 1900 or 1899.
Question: Was *he* the Attwood?

Action: Check military records for an Attwood with biographical details as known.

Fact: "He was born and grew up in England, after leaving school apprenticed for two years, then joined a troop ship and spent several months in the Mediterranean area and France. He returned to England and joined an Army regiment with whom he saw service with a great deal of travel."

Question: What did he do as an apprentice? Was this the British Army?

Action: Search immigration records again for just after First World War. Write for British military records.

Fact: "His father was retired, still alive, in good health, in his late 70s in England. His mother died from shock, following total demolishment of her home in a bombing raid early in the war."

Question: Where was their home?

Action: Search casualty records in Britain. Start with large cities that had the most bombing during the first years of the war.

Fact: "He had hoped to be able to plan divorce proceedings while back in Canada at the time of your birth but found there was not sufficient time."

Question: I knew he had eventually married my birth mother, so where and when had the divorce taken place?

Action: Reference to divorce proceedings strong enough to make it worthwhile finding divorce records after 1943, but before 1950, as my brother or sister had been born about that time.

Fact: I had been placed in a Mothercraft home while my birth parents sorted out the best plan for me.

Questions: Did Mothercraft keep files? Where was the home?

Action: Contact Mothercraft and find out some of their history? Where were early files and how open were they now? Could I find and contact anyone who worked there at the time of my placement?

Fact: "Your adoption was arranged privately by a doctor who appears to have known both your birth parents and adoptive parents."

Question: Could this be a classmate of my father's?

Action: Contact a close friend who was a classmate, the only one still alive, and simply enlist his help. Contact children of other deceased classmates. Could any of the doctors be placed in Barrie during the summer of 1942?

Fact: "Your birth mother was 30 years old, single, born in Ontario."

Question: Where was she born in 1911 or 1912?

Action: Search for records for both her birth certificate and her parents' death certificates and wills. Search city directories to try to find their place of residence. They may not have known about me, but perhaps I could find people who knew one of their three daughters and thus trace her present whereabouts.

Fact: "She was raised in a stable, comfortable environment, where there had been a lot of music and church involvement."

Question: What church?

Action: Supposition, but since her parents had emigrated from England, they were likely Anglican. Therefore a search of church records for births, marriages, deaths would be in order. Since she was a churchgoer, and I had been with my parents for two weeks before being placed in the home, might I have been baptized — in Barrie?

Fact: "She completed high school, went on to graduate and then to work at her profession."
Question: Where did she go to school? Does graduate mean from high school? The term "profession" would likely indicate a university degree or perhaps a nursing diploma. What would be termed a "profession" in 1942?
Action: Find towns where Attwoods lived, search high school records and yearbooks. Contact universities for female graduates around 1935. This could also be done for hospitals, likely in southern Ontario. What hospitals had nursing courses at that time?

Fact: "Her father, in his late 70's, had been born in England and came to Canada as a young man."
Question: When did he immigrate?
Action: Search of immigration records for the 1890s.

Fact: "He found work with a large Canadian company and remained with them until his retirement."
Question: What, in 1942, would be defined as "a large Canadian Company"? Does the use of Canadian as an adjective imply a company with branches across the country, such as a bank, insurance company, or transportation business?
Action: Difficult, but it would be possible to isolate the

major companies that fit this description and research their employment and pension records.

Fact: "Your birth mother had three older sisters, all married with children. They had completed high school, worked in offices prior to their marriages."
Question: Where are they now?
Action: Check city directories for family with four girls.

Fact: "An older brother had graduated from University."
Question: Where is he now?
Action: This was a very powerful lead, for he would have the same family name if I had been given her maiden name. Check city directories looking at professions that would entail a university education, especially if four girls in family. Check university records for a male Attwood who graduated before 1935.

After reading and rereading the information I took the dog for a long overdue outing. As we walked the paths of the university campus in the clear cold of a February afternoon, I thought about my birth mother and father. They had stepped forward a little, emerging from the shadows; they were becoming real to me. I knew I would never be satisfied until I found them. I was not looking for a permanent relationship, but I longed to meet them, to hear their voices, to find out more about the family, about my background. Were they still alive? I didn't want to contemplate the possibility that I might be too late.

All I had were the barest of facts. How much more had the social worker read through before she compiled this biographical précis of the characters in a tiny drama in the middle of wartime? What had she left out? Were these clues hidden in the non-identifying information enough to discover names and addresses? They would have to be, for there was nothing more.

The arrival of my non-identifying information ushered in a much more positive phase of my life. The past two years had been overlaid by simmering anger and frustration. Now there was a focus for my energy, and hope replaced desperation. My search was now self-directed. I had accepted the fact that nobody was going to give me any information just for the asking. Those who knew wouldn't speak — and those who were willing to speak knew so very little! I would have to scrounge for every additional item of information. I was also determined that never again would I give away the fact, when inquiring for data, that I was a searching adoptee.

The obvious first step was to check my father's military records here in Canada. Was there a file concerning an Attwood who was born in England in 1899 or 1900, who had served in the British forces in the First World War and in the Canadian forces in the Second? If there was, I was essentially on my way, for then I would have his first name and a known address (albeit one that was forty years old), and then it would simply be a matter of straightforward searching through the paper trail, telephone books and directories. If an Attwood with his biographical details was not to be found in the military archives, then Attwood must be my mother's name. I would then have to trace her family. It would mean a long process of elimination, but it could be done. There would be success in either response from the Department of National Defence.

Did one just write for access to these records, or was one invited to flip through thousands of file cards? This was still before one could count on information being available at the touch of a computer key. I even thought that if Attwood was eliminated as his name, I might be able to go to Ottawa and work my way through the files for men in my father's birth years simply looking for his biographical details, since there could not be many who had served in both the Canadian and British armed forces. Would I have access to this information wholesale and be able to work out his identify simply by letting my fingers do the walking?

I wrote to the Archives of the Department of National Defence, and gave them his biographical details, mentioning the name Attwood, and just to be safe, mentioning Bainbridge as well.

Within two or three weeks I had a response to my letter. There was no record of an Attwood or Bainbridge with my father's military background. Therefore, I was searching for my mother's maiden name. Battle lines were drawn and my strategy was mapped out. Putting my father aside for two years, I set off to find my mother. Several paths stretched out before me and all could be followed simultaneously, until I found one that looked as if it would produce results.

Track number one: Find out where the Attwood families are in Ontario by using city/town directories and telephone books. Voters' rolls would be useful here, as would tax records and census forms. Newspaper files with their records of births, marriages and deaths would also provide information. If there were several locations where there were clusters of Attwoods, a visit to cemeteries would give an indication of ages and times of death. Sometimes this route is faster than poring over newspapers. All you have to do is find a headstone, and all cemeteries have directories.

Track number two: Search records of universities and schools, also church records.

After following these courses I would, with luck, eventually find out where she came from, where she went and whom she married. None of this was simple or straightforward. It represented hours of slogging hard work. But how long would it take? I didn't have all the time in the world. She was getting on in years.

A search may be compared to a ball of wool after a playful kitten has had an evening with it. The threads are broken and tangled; the whole scene is one of confusion. The wool must be organized into a useable ball. The task is to untangle the information — and not only to tie the broken pieces together, but to re-unite them in their original sequence.

Conducting a search can be confusing. There are clues but they don't fit together. You may suddenly be overwhelmed with ideas, for frequently one brainwave leads you to another angle of thought, which in turn triggers yet another, which leads you off on another tangent. I used to keep pencil and paper in strategic places all over the house just to jot down various reflections and ideas as they came. Your mind becomes overloaded. You are sure you could never forget an idea or a fact and then a well-meaning friend chooses that moment to telephone and ask how things are going, or to beseech you to bake a pie for the curling club supper. Poof!

Each of these ideas, concepts and filaments of specu-
lation must be clarified, then separated and broken down
into workable components. Threads must be reluctantly
put aside, but not forgotten, while others are followed.
You do not always see the logical steps to following
through on an idea. Then in the middle of the night or
after talking with friends, you see another facet of an idea
that must be explored. You go back and forth, picking up
strands here and there — one that seems irrelevant today
may become critically important in several months.
Nothing must be discarded, only filed away.

Time can be a chief frustration. You write letters, make
inquiries and then wait, and *wait*, for the answers. It
proves absolutely vital to keep a journal, writing down
when things were done, and noting even the smallest
pieces of information, for as in a jigsaw puzzle, the most
unlikely pieces will interlock. Everything must be kept.
Copies of letters written, notes of telephone calls (what
was asked, what was said in reply; reactions, yours and
those of the person you were speaking to). Was a question suspiciously brushed off? Did someone come to
their door, and a point get lost? Did you sidetrack them
before they had finished one idea? Any number of things
can act as a block to communication. The file will grow.
You refer to it over and over until the papers become
dog-eared. You read and reread, constantly looking for
something that might have been missed the first time or
the twentieth time. Sometimes things take on a different
meaning in the light of a new discovery. Perhaps something as simple as a good night's sleep or a holiday lets
you come back to the work able to see old, seemingly
useless information in a new light.

Above all, I had to be organized. I had two notebooks. One was simply a journal where I wrote down the date and everything that I did that day. I also used this notebook to scrawl things that people said to me on the phone, or to note the receipt or sending of a letter. If it was the receipt of a letter, I made a cross note on the page of the date when I had written the letter to which this was the reply. Chronology of events is important. I also made a note here of what I was going to do with the information. It is surprising how information overload sets in and you find yourself thinking, "There was a good reason I did this, but I can't remember it!"

The second was a three-ring notebook divided into sections. The first section was entitled KNOWN, GIVEN INFORMATION. I ran four columns across the top under the headings *Date, Source, Information, Comments/Action.* I broke down the details of the so-called non-identifying information under sub-headings *Birth, Location, Mother, Father, Birth mother's family, Birth father's family* (again sub-headed *Mother, Father, Family*). Then each time I spoke to someone I recorded the information in the appropriate column.

The next step was to read over all this information and brainstorm, privately at first. You ask yourself how you could use this information, how you could expand it, where you could go to expand these details, what other facts you could glean from it, and then jot down your conclusions under the Comments/Action column. The notebook is best kept at hand when you are talking to sympathetic family or friends, to give focus to your ideas as you jot down their information in the appropriate places. I used colored pens — anything for clarity. I went back to this list again and again as I discovered more links.

The second section I set up was for HEARSAY. I entered all sorts of little bits and pieces from my history — the famous "someone said" comments. You can't dismiss them, but you can't get them mixed up with known facts. I set this up as I did the first section.

Thirdly, SEARCH INFORMATION. Here the columns are *Date, Information, Comments, Source.* This section grows and grows. Even though a lot of it may turn out to be irrelevant, it does at least give you the feeling of having accomplished something. You might hear from some dear old soul on March 29 that she just remembered that her sister had a neighbour who worked with someone who might be able to supply some biographical details. It got entered. You find out her sister's name and track her down if you think it is worthwhile. "Do if desperate" goes on notes such as these, for one does have to set priorities.

When I took an action on a certain item, I noted the date in the comments column and kept checking back to remind myself what had been done. This served as a reminder if I needed to write a follow-up letter. When an item could be eliminated, I put an X beside it. But I didn't strike it out. You never know when you might need it again. It was so important to put down *everything,* whether it was so earth-shattering that I could not imagine ever forgetting it, or so insignificant that I was sure it could never be of any importance. It might be, and searches are built on mights and maybes and what-ifs!

Fourthly, TO DO. This tied in with the Comments/Action column in sections one and two. There occasionally was some duplication here with Comments/Action, but sometimes you get an inspiration that isn't directly related to a clue on the list. It had to be written down somewhere.

Finally, a section for FAMILY TREES. I didn't skimp on paper, using a separate page for each tree. It is amazing how many people you find in the course of a search. Over the years of my inquiries I found four distinct Attwood families in Ontario. People refer to their cousin, or an uncle, and if you can visualize the relationships it keeps the generations straight. Starting with my contact's name, I added on any members of the family they described. The Genealogical Research Library in London, Ontario, has an excellent booklet on building one's family tree. I noted sources and added names as they came along. This may be more important than you know, even if you are relatively sure that it isn't your birth family that you are mapping out, for you can learn a lot through the process of elimination.

It comes down to how to organize hundreds, if not thousands, of bits of information without allowing them to become unwieldy. I had a whole file drawer for letters and kept copies of everything. When a reply came in I clipped it to the original letter.

There was an overpowering temptation to charge ahead when I got hold of a hot tip or a brilliant idea. I found that organization is more than an exercise, it is the key to sanity!

5

INTO THE
LABYRINTH

*There appears to be no apparent reason for
secrecy and for attempts to cut adopted
people from their origins. What we are, is
what our parents and forebears have been
over many generations.*

John Triseliotis, *Adoptees in Search of
Their Origins*

FOR THE NEXT year and a half I focussed on one thing and
one thing only: my search. I wonder now how it was
possible for me to find so much time, for my life as a
working wife and mother continued on a relatively normal keel. The fifteen minutes while the potatoes boiled
gave me time to make a phone call; notes replaced the
novel to be read in the bath. A note pad sat by my bed
waiting for the ideas that came in the small hours. I
walked the dog on the university campus almost every
day and would tie her inside the front doors of the library
while I scanned the births and deaths in the newspaper
files for an hour or so. I realized just how much time I

spent there when one day my husband and I left the house to run some errands. We left Enika, our black Lab mix, tied outside in the sunshine, and when we returned an hour later we found nothing but a frayed rope. All dog lovers know the worry and trepidation that hits when a beloved pet disappears. Calls to the police, the vet, a slow whistling tour of town resulted in nothing. Four hours later we received a call from the university librarian. A black-and-white dog had slipped into the library and was holding the security man at bay behind a desk! Where else could her mistress be but at the library?

I hoped to find the announcement of my sibling's birth, which I *knew* was in a Toronto paper. If the divorce hadn't gone through by 1942, and my father was in the forces, my birth parents would probably not have married until some time in the period 1945–1947, and therefore the birth would have been announced somewhere between 1946 and 1949 — those were the years my second cousin was in training. I had never realized the extent of the post-war baby boom until I began searching the birth records of those years! The great pitfall of searching through old newspapers is that headlines catch your eye and it is very easy to become sidetracked by the news of the day. Great accounts of victory in Europe, a touching story of a serviceman who had been reported killed in action but reappeared on the doorstep unaware that his family thought him dead. These were insights into a world long gone, the world into which I had been born. I skimmed each page of the B.M.D. (Births, Marriages, Deaths) — the Marriages for my parents' wedding announcement, and the Deaths in case one of my maternal grandparents had died during that crucial period. Any mention of any Attwood would have been helpful. This exercise, which ended up stretching from February to November, 1984, profited me nothing. I saw the name Attwood only once in all my search of the Toronto newspapers. They were not big city people, this Attwood clan.

Toronto had three major papers in those days, the *Globe and Mail*, which was universally read, and the *Telegram* and the *Toronto Daily Star*, which were radically divided by politics. Our university had microfilms only for the *Globe and Mail*, so I spent hours and hours during each visit to Toronto in the reference section of the public library going through the files of the other two papers. At one point the librarians went on strike and the research library was closed, so it was over to the library of the University of Toronto.

Microfiche machines have characters unto themselves. Each one has its own particular foibles, squeaks and mannerisms. Each reader seemed to have a favourite, and I very quickly learned that one had to be careful not to infringe on their territory, as at a church one has to make sure not to take someone else's pew. Several times I was interrupted by a polite "Excuse me, this is my machine," which is only slightly better than feeling a hard stare on the back of the neck. I never discovered what you were actually to do when you came into the library and saw a vacant machine.

However, I soon discovered the importance of having a machine that I knew and understood. There was one machine at the university library that I never used, even if it was the only vacant one — it had a voracious appetite and a mind of its own. I became a regular in the three libraries and staked out my territory.

One of the frustrations of skimming newspapers on microfilm, as contrasted with careful reading or research, is that libraries limit the number of reels you can have in your possession at any one time. Four was the magic number, as I remember. You had to fill in a form for each set, take the form to the desk, wait your turn, wait for the reels to be found and wait your turn to pick them up, only to go through the whole process again and again. Knowing that you could cover a whole week of newspapers in the time you stood waiting didn't make it any easier. My type A personality was learning the truth of the old adage that patience is a virtue.

My first foray into newspapers yielded no clues. I decided that I could perhaps use my time more wisely on another track. Shortly before this marathon session in the library I had talked to Dr. Andy, a classmate of my father's, and of the doctor who delivered me. (By this time I had identified that doctor. Unfortunately, he had died several years before.) This wonderful gentleman was a tower of strength throughout my search. In frustration I had said to him, "You *must* know something!" He replied gently that he and my father were close friends, and that he and his wife had rejoiced with my parents when I arrived but had never thought of asking for any details. "I'm sure your father would have told me, had I asked, but the important thing was that you were with them." His guidance helped me to keep things in perspective. He, too, said that he thought the name started with B and was a short name.

My cousin, in another chat, said she thought my birth family had gone out west, but if my birth father had been in "The San" and had died in Toronto, they obviously did not stay long. So I moved to the other bank of microfiche readers and started tackling Toronto city directories.

Many Canadian cities do have directories, but they will be known by the name of their publisher. They are usually found at the main reference library or at the city hall. There are two sets of directories for Toronto. The *Bower's Directory* is published each year and the listings are based on telephone numbers rather than names. The more useful directory, from the point of view of a search, is *Might's Directory*. The listings are by name and will give the address and frequently the profession of the individual. There are also listings by address, so if you have that information you can work back to the name of the individual living there. This is a very powerful tool, for you may discover that a birth relative lived on a certain street, or in a certain area. With judicious use of the directory, a city map and knowledge of the person's profession, you could discover a name.

I knew that my father had been with an insurance company, and I went through the directories looking for Attwoods listed as practising this profession, and through the Bs looking for short names and Bainbridges, but letting my eyes skim all of them. One February morning I thought I had hit the jackpot. I had found an Arthur H. Burt, a new, proud parent in the July, 1945, birth announcements in the *Toronto Daily Star*; cross-checking with the directory, I found that he was also employed by an insurance company. Now the fun began, moving back and forth through the years. He disappeared from the directory in 1950 (which would fit with the move west) and reappeared in 1962, where he stayed until he disappeared again in 1971. A bit late for my father's death by "known" information, but then I had no direct proof of the date of his death. Moving over to the current phone books I discovered there was an A.H. at the same address that had been in the 1971 directory. Was this a son, a younger brother? Still being nervous about direct phone calls, I decided to track down his biographical details through the military archives.

First thing when I returned home I wrote to the Department of Defence in Ottawa. Their files can become an important touchstone. One thing about patriotism is that the chances of a Canadian male within certain age brackets having served in the forces is very high. The army never discards its records, and they are surprisingly accessible. It is another case of the contradictions in the laws pertaining to open and closed records. Anyone can write for the military history of anyone else; everything is on open record: transfers, decorations, mention in dispatches and misdemeanours. Reputations could be ruined — and all it takes is a letter.

The reply when it came several weeks later dug a definite grave for that lead. A.H. Burt had been born in 1916. Wrong man!

There are a surprisingly large number of Bs in the insurance business. For each one I went through the same procedure as above. I looked for disappearance and reappearance in the directory, and then checked with the military archives. I am indebted to an unseen civil servant, Francine, whose last name I never knew. I talked to her many, many times. It is always better to get a name of a helpful individual and then go back to him or her. This is doubly important when one is working on long-distance telephone, at peak rates, for it saves so much time in explanations. It also sets up a personal contact that is amazingly good for your morale. Just to have someone ask "How is it going? What's new?" is wonderful. In the end you *don't* save any money on long-distance calls, because you want to answer their questions and they want to hear! It is also possible that a sympathetic person who spends her life with archives will have useful ideas for other places to look, especially if they become "hooked" on your search. I had consulted Francine so often that I eventually confessed all to her. She became even more friendly and helpful, fascinated with it all and eager to be of assistance.

In the city directory I found an "X" Atwood who worked at Mothercraft — a real coincidence. This might have explained why I was placed in a Mothercraft home after spending two weeks with my mother. By this time I had discovered that I was not adopted until November (dating it by another cousin who was married the weekend I "arrived," and who remembered that my parents couldn't come to her wedding), and that meant that I had been in the home fourteen weeks. Was that normal? What was the hold-up? If it wasn't the usual course of events, then a staff member, if I could locate one, might not have forgotten it. However, there was no record of a sister who was a nurse, for according to the non-identifying information they had all worked in offices. On the other hand, could this woman have worked in the office of the Mothercraft home? Could there be a mistake in the non-identifying information? Round and round it went.

Each discovery prompted another bombardment of questions and more jottings. I found a "Y" Atwood who was a stenographer with a life insurance company. Could my mother have had a job with the same insurance company as my father? I had interpreted the phrase in the non-identifying information — "she completed high school, went on to graduate and then to work at her profession" — to mean that she graduated from an institution beyond high school, likely a university since the term *profession* was used to describe her field of employment. The word would not have been used for a stenographer's job. A sister perhaps? A lead to be followed. She disappeared from the Toronto directory in 1946, but a "Y" (same first name as Attwood the stenographer) Bailey had a baby in July of 1946. Had "Y" Attwood fallen in love with Mr. Bailey? Perhaps a call to the personnel records of the insurance company was in order. I never followed up that lead, as I took a different track, but it is an example of the convoluted thinking that is necessary.

One basic search technique is simply to go to the current telephone book and start calling people with the name for which you are searching. This is not as straightforward as it sounds. You can't just telephone a stranger and say, "Excuse me, I was adopted forty years ago and am searching for my birth parents. They have your surname and I wonder if you know anything about them?" Life would be so much simpler if you *could* do it that way, but it would show a total lack of sensitivity and awareness of your birth parents' right to confidentiality.

My story was that I was doing genealogical research into my family history. I was pessimistic enough that I didn't really believe I would find anyone who actually was part of my family, and foolish enough not to have mapped out what I would say if I did.

To give my eyes a break from directories, and my back a change from sitting, I did some of my calling from the pay phone in the foyer of the Toronto library. I laid out a row of quarters, wedged the corner of my notebook under the phone and prepared for a half hour of calling. Imagine my shock when on my second call, after I had given the gentleman the biographical outline, he said, "The university graduate was my father!" I was literally speechless. He went on to say that his father had died but his aunts were still alive. Hopefully, I asked if he would give me their addresses. No, he didn't feel that he could give that information to a stranger. So near and yet so far! But in the course of the conversation he had mentioned his aunt's last name, and the small town in western Ontario where she lived. I jotted both down. It looked very promising, as I understood that my people had some connection with that particular area of Ontario. I thanked him profusely, hung up, wrote his name and phone number in big red letters in my book, shoved the remaining quarters into my pocket and rushed off to consult the phone book of the town he had mentioned. His aunt's name was there. I was learning that people inadvertently do give clues and that it was necessary to listen "between the lines."

I never had to get back to my security-conscious gentleman, for I did get in touch with his aunt on the first call. She was a charming lady, with none of her nephew's reservations about talking to a stranger. She was most helpful and became for some time an important link in the building-up of family trees. On the whole it was the older people who were more willing to talk and to give information — a sad commentary on the state of our society. This first call was somewhat traumatic. What if this by chance turned out to be my mother? However, very early on in the conversation she mentioned her husband, who was still alive, and thus she became just another name on a family tree, albeit a helpful one. She filled me in on the family history as she knew it and then gave me her father's phone number. (Nephew had never mentioned that his grandfather was still alive.) I called him and had a most interesting chat with a marvellous old man, but he was unable to make any link with any of the biographical details that fitted my family.

I sent her the list of all the possible Attwoods from the Toronto phone book of the 1940s. Elimination is as important as direct contacts. One of the names was her uncle, who had been killed in the North Atlantic in 1942. She would have given me the telephone number of his daughter, but I felt that she herself was my most important contact from that generation, and that her cousin would not have been able to add anything concrete. In fact, this was not really very astute of me. As I subsequently learned, different members of the same family can have quite different memories, and it is worth speaking to everyone you can. It is fascinating to follow families, for one becomes interested in them as people, even though there is no direct relationship. She identified another Attwood on my list as having moved to Detroit, where he lived until he died in the 1960s. He had two sons who still lived in the States. And so, two more names eliminated.

Another contact lived in British Columbia; her father was on my list. One more eliminated. This lady sent me an outline of her family tree that enabled me to eliminate several other names I had gleaned from here and there. I had enough information now to tie many of my assorted names together. It was amazing to me that total strangers would react so positively and productively to my search. They had no way of knowing how much they helped.

From March until May of 1984 I was back in Quebec, writing letters and making countless long-distance telephone calls. The Barrie Public Library told me that there were no Attwoods in the city directory for 1934, 1937, or 1942. Ergo, my mother did not come originally from Barrie; if she had, she or at least her parents would have been listed.

Librarians are extremely helpful people if you make a point of calling in quiet times, or when you know there is a raging snowstorm in the area. They will quell their boredom, or take time out from routine tasks to do the most unbelievable things for you. I found that if I made my request and then asked when I could call back, they would usually say to give them half an hour. Half an hour later they were there with the answer or were very apologetic if they hadn't managed to get it done or to have found anything. This was certainly better than waiting for a letter, which might have got tied up in the incoming or outgoing mail!

In March I had another flurry of ideas. My adoptive father had been connected with a lodge, and somewhere along the line I remembered hearing that my birth father had also been a lodge member. Could it have been the same organization? I managed to contact an old lodge brother of my father's. His niece answered the phone and told me that he had had a stroke and was very confused. However, she said she would make the effort to speak to him to see if he knew of any other members who might have been in the insurance business and might be able to make some connections.

Back to Dr. Andy again to inquire about names. Bainbridge didn't ring a bell with him at all. However, he came up with the idea of contacting the sanatorium in Gravenhurst for their records. He told me that my birth father had been a lieutenant or a captain during the Second World War. This reinforced in me the wisdom of getting back to my contacts. Dr. Andy had not mentioned this fact before, not because he was withholding information but because he just hadn't thought of it. The interesting thing was that, although he said my parents had never mentioned any details about my family background to him, he did, somehow, know this fact. So the topic had certainly come up.

Wondering if perhaps they were still in Gravenhurst, I called the Gravenhurst library to see if they had a Bainbridge or an Attwood on their rolls. After my reception at government offices, I tended to use libraries whenever I could. They seemed so much less threatening. I thought that if my mother was a university graduate who loved books, the chances of her belonging to the local public library were strong. From this call came the best line of my whole search. The librarian turned from the phone and called out to a colleague, "Myrtle, do we have any Bainbridges or Attwoods who read?" A muffled reply indicated that there was a Bainbridge who lived in a senior citizens' home and the librarian very kindly gave me her name.

One does not just pick up the phone to call to ask "are you my mother?" I called the Department of Veterans' Affairs to find out if a Mrs. Bainbridge of Gravenhurst was getting a pension, and if her maiden name had been Attwood. Dead end. There had been two Bainbridges in the forces, one an officer in the army, and the other in the air force, but neither had dependants in Gravenhurst. So the armed-forces Bainbridges did not fit the biographical details of my father. One more item of information could be eliminated.

I then called our college chaplain to see how one would go about contacting a parish priest in another part of the country. If my father had indeed been in the sanatorium in Gravenhurst, my family might still belong to a church in Gravenhurst. This was a lead that I did not have to follow through.

Spring came, with new growth, new life, new hope. Despite my careful organization, the thread of the Mothercraft lead had got lost; a rereading of my notebook brought it into view again. A call to their office left me empty-handed; their records went back only to 1960. They did give me the name of a retired nurse who had worked there in 1942. More help, and another lead.

With spring came another business trip to Ontario and another visit with my friend in Waterloo, who had been the recipient of my outpourings after the great discovery. After her children had been tucked into bed, she and her husband and I sat around the kitchen table and brainstormed. Friends can be a tremendous help in getting new ideas. On the other hand, you must be very careful not to burden your friends. It is your search, your drive, your obsession; not theirs. Four hundred miles is a good buffer, and good friends that you don't see often are usually willing to help when you do get together. The ideas came fast and furious. My notes from that evening are a scrawl. My birth father had been in the process of getting a divorce . . . there must be records somewhere. The home town of his first wife was known (how, I can't remember), and since divorce was relatively rare in those days could I find (tactfully) anyone who knew her, or of the divorce? If he had worked for an insurance company his wife would probably be getting a pension from the company. Could one obtain access to these records? Of course I didn't have a surname, and that would make things slightly more difficult. It would be simply asking people I knew from that city if they knew anyone who had been married for fifteen years, whose husband had divorced her after the war. I took to heart the adage that "the impossible just takes a little longer."

How does one get information? We came up with the idea of calling the *Globe and Mail*'s legal department to ask how divorce records were made public. Osgoode Hall could tell me where the records might be stored and how public they were. It was a long, long night and the coffee pot was refilled several times. I remember that conversation so vividly. One of us would steal a glance at the clock and observe that we really had to go to bed, another would come up with a fresh idea and we would be off again.

The next day was just as bad, or good. After spending the morning interviewing prospective camp staff at the University of Waterloo, I headed down the road to the University of Guelph for a lunchtime interview and then to the home of the second cousin who had told me so

much the year before. Another brainstorming session —
different people, different generation, different slant, different ideas. We started looking at the whole military
angle. If my father had lived in London, Ontario, he
would very likely have joined the Royal Canadian Regiment, which was based in that city. My cousin looked at
the phone and said, "Call now." That conversation was
one for the books! The poor buck private on the switch-
board didn't know anything about archives. I was
shunted from office to office and back again to finally
find myself talking to the regimental museum. The army,
in the person of the poor chap on duty, was nonplussed.
He couldn't imagine how I hoped to track down someone whose name I didn't even know. For that matter,
neither did I. The only idea I did have was that their
records would indicate previous military service, and
since my father had also served in the First World War,
that would give me another list of names to trace.

"Surely," I asked, "you must have a list of all the men
who were in the regiment before and during the Second
World War?"

"Well, yes."

"Could I come to look at the list?"

"But you don't know his name."

"True, but I have some ideas."

"What good would that do?"

At that point I didn't have the energy to try to explain.
I thanked the little man, and made a note that when I was
really desperate I would take up that trail again. In theory,
it was a trail I should have followed, given the knowledge I had then. In practice, it would have been time
wasted, for that was not my father's regiment. *But it*

might have been. I don't know why I didn't take it more seriously at the time — maybe I had mentally reviewed various improbabilities and just didn't record the process. I had to remember to use my notebook to record discarded ideas, *and* why I had decided not to follow them up.

A second idea that we came up with was that my first name, Alleyne, was unusual enough to be a clue. Mary's husband told me that it was also a surname, so perhaps Alleyne was one of my parents' surnames, and Attwood the other. My birth parents *had* given me a name, although surely they knew my adoptive parents would change it to one of their own choosing. In such circumstances, wouldn't they have given me names that were significant, if only to themselves? Perhaps they thought, romantically, that if as an adult I ever found out my original name, it would provide me with clues to my background. Clutching at straws, we spent some considerable time dealing with that idea.

With the London phone book at hand, I checked for Attwoods, and called one at random. I told him that I was searching for family information, in particular trying to find a man who had been born in 1899 or 1900 in England. I gave him the full known biographical information. Still not sure if Attwood was my mother's or father's name, I also described my birth mother's background, as another Attwood. He said that nothing rang a bell, but he would contact other members of the family. During the conversation he gave me a great deal of information about his family, which game me more names, leads, ideas.

Back in Toronto, I looked up Alleyne in the phone

book. Much to my surprise, there was a long list. Picking one at random, I called, and was greeted by a very warm Caribbean voice, that replied to my query, "I don't think you are related to us." Apparently most of the ancestors of the Alleynes in Ontario were from Barbados — slaves who had been given the name of their owner at the time of emancipation. A year or two later when visiting Barbados, I followed up the original Alleyne family and discovered that the name Alleyne is a medieval form of Allen — my present surname! Truth is stranger than fiction.

After this interesting elimination of a hopeful lead, I called the retired nurse from the Mothercraft home whose name had been given to me somewhere along the line. This lady was in her seventies, obviously lived alone, and was happy to spend time chatting. She told me all about the early days of Mothercraft. But she didn't have the specific knowledge that was needed. She was able to give me the phone number of the Attwood nurse who had been there at the time I was. I considered this a very significant lead, for what better place to put a child than in a home where there was a sympathetic relative?

So, sitting in a friend's beautiful winterized sun porch, surrounded by flowers, I dialled a number that I hoped would put a speedy end to my search. I gave her my now well-rehearsed story, but was disappointed. She asked me the spelling of the last name. My hasty reading had wasted my time and hers; her name was spelled Atwood and she knew nothing about a two-"t" Attwood child.

Back to the archives, this time in Barrie. I took the precaution of telephoning first, and saved a trip, for all their birth records were deposited at Queen's Park in Toronto. There seems to be no way of telling which small towns keep their records and which take advantage of the large storage facilities of the provincial government. Archivists are a very helpful, willing group of people. If you are working from a distance, they will usually look things up for you. They checked the 1940s city directories for me, but that proved to be another dead end.

Another series of letters, this time to the Toronto Attwoods that I hadn't been able to contact by phone. In this day and age of word processors, it is a temptation to churn out letters by the yard, but unless you own a true letter-quality printer, it isn't worth it. If I was contacting a stranger for personal information, I could not give the impression that I was approaching him or her in an impersonal way. I was asking busy individuals to take time to write to me, and I knew I must show in every way possible that I recognized this, and that they and their information were important to me. The form of the letter must say it, too. I always enclosed a self-addressed stamped envelope with each request for information.

During the search, I remembered to get back at regular intervals to strong leads — people who indicated a willingness to help. I knew they might come up with new ideas, or old memories may have surfaced since the last time I was in touch with them. As my contact in London wrote, "I haven't thought much about the family, but with your interest all sorts of things are coming back." People may hesitate to call; I was the initiator, so it was up to me to keep the lines of communication open.

A call to the Ministry of Defence Archives confirmed that they would try to help me out, if I could give them what information I had. Archivists can do the most incredible things with small items of information and computer files. If they couldn't find anything the first time, I kept feeding them with significant information as I discovered it. One tiny clue may have been just what they needed to unearth a treasure trove.

I wrote a letter to the Children's Aid asking for information about legal grounds for a possible appeal for identifying information, and received the following reply:

> To my knowledge there is no appeal for other than medical reasons open to adoptees. In fact, a recent Court decision denied a 55 year old adoptee the right to any information about birth family stating there is no provision for this in the legislation. As a result our Ministry is not releasing any information while allowing individual Children's Aid Societies to set their own policy — our Society is continuing to share non-identifying information.

My reaction was simply a somewhat sarcastic, "Gee — thanks a lot!" It is frighteningly easy to be overwhelmed with the absolute inanity of the whole scene. Our society is now set up to try to deal with so many problems. We have counselling procedures for literally everyone — marriage counselling for marriages gone wrong, youth counselling and programs for "youth at risk," special programs for bright learning-disabled youngsters, Alcoholics Anonymous for people who have come to rely on the bottle to solve their problems; the list goes on and on. Why, then, has there been total blindness to the plight of the well over 300,000 people in Canada who find themselves in genealogical confusion because they have been trapped in the "as if born" corner of the adoption triangle!

6

HIRE A DETECTIVE?
NEVER!

Tolkien tells us that all fairy stories must
have a recovery and consolation at the
end — the evil doer is punished and the
universe is put into order. But in the
adoption story there is no evil to be
punished — for there is no villain — all
the characters thought they were acting
"in the best interest" of the baby at the
time of adoption.

Betty Jean Lifton, *Lost and Found:*
The Adoption Experience

IT WAS TIME for a jump shift of direction in my search.
My maternal birth grandparents had to have been
buried somewhere in Ontario. Perhaps it would be possible to discover where they had lived through cemetery
or land grants records. The Genealogical Research Library in London, Ontario, does wide-spectrum searches
and provincial land-record searches for a fee. I did not
have to avail myself of this service, but certainly it would
have been a tack to take in the future, had it been neces-

sary. They will also (for a fee) do searches of city and town directories — certainly a valuable service for those unable to travel to the town in question.

I gave the representative at the G.R.L. my usual spiel about looking for family, and was immediately asked if I was adopted. It's our lack of information that gives us away.

May. Leaves on the trees, warm days, time passing — and I was getting nowhere fast. This was a difficult period, knowing I would have to take three months off for camp with so many loose ends still hanging. I gave up sleep, my family saw less and less of me and I kept working. More calls — I was able to contact the daughter of the doctor who delivered me. We had an old-fashioned chat, for I had last seen her in 1957 when we had gone on the father-daughter ski weekend. Now at last "the girls talked," but twenty years too late. She knew nothing, except to say that her father sometimes had been on call to the hospital in Barrie during the summer since their cottage was nearby. This confirmed what I had gathered somewhere along the line: that he indeed had delivered me. She had kept in contact with another old classmate of our fathers' and was willing to call him for me. She did so, but he had no information.

Is it better to telephone, or to write? I found that telephoning was better, because you knew your message had been received and you got an immediate response. You were not dependent on their getting around to writing you back. A disadvantage is that telephoning doesn't give the source time to think. To people who were close to my adoptive parents I wrote first, explaining carefully what I was doing and my reasons for doing so, and reassuring them of my love and loyalty to my adoptive parents. If they had not replied after three weeks, I called. But for more casual, impersonal inquiries, I found the telephone to be best. If they couldn't remember anything, I asked them to think about it and call me back collect, or to allow me to call them back some time in the future. A search is not cheap, but it is cheaper than hiring a private detective, who is not emotionally involved.

With all the correspondence that was coming in from my contacts I was now able to start building up three proper family trees. Even though I knew that these people were in no way related to me, my detailed knowledge of them and their relationship or non-relationship one to another became absolutely crucial to the final outcome, because it furthered the process of elimination. There were only so many people bearing this family name in Ontario — how fortunate I was to be dealing with an unusual name!

With each letter and each additional fact my determination grew. An example of a letter to me: "My grandparents came from England around 1900 and settled in Glace Bay. My grandparents had three boys and four girls. The sons, like their father, all worked and retired from the coal mines. Sorry that's all the information I can give you." This was written in pencil on half a sheet of lined paper. Somewhere out there was the same type of information on *my* misty family.

Just to keep the lines of communication open I called Children's Aid in Toronto again to see if there was anything at all, any tidbit of information, that they could squeeze out of their files — that they perchance had missed the first time, or that another social worker might decide was non-identifying, but to no avail. I thought they sounded somewhat apologetic this time. They suggested that I place an advertisement in the *Toronto Star's* special column for adoption searchers. The irony of this piece of advice took my breath away, coming from the organization that was holding in its files all the information I needed. If it was all right for me to obtain the information by advertising, why was it not all right just to give it to me directly? It seemed that they too believed that I had a natural and moral right to know. They just didn't have the *legal* right to tell me! It was ludicrous, infuriating and heart-breaking.

During the summer of 1984 I worked, and waited for information. I kept hoping for results from the advertisements in the *Star* and in the Lost Trails column of *Legion* magazine, but I was disappointed.

A lawyer friend came to the camp to visit, and I took advantage of a quiet evening by the fire to pump her for information. Her contention was that no records are completely sealed, that it is just a case of finding someone who has the right to look into them, and persuading him, or more likely her, to do it. Where there's a will, there's a way. Time and time again the underhandedness of searching bothered me, but it comes down to your own attitude to rights. Which is the greater evil, the situation with which we are faced, or the "little white lies" that we must tell?

My friend confirmed that divorce records are open to the public, but they are difficult to locate, and I never did manage to do so, despite numerous calls to the Supreme Court of Ontario and a trip to the Supreme Court in

Ottawa. The Senate has records but only up to the year 1931. At the end of August I had a letter from the Supreme Court records office, listing the local registry offices throughout Canada where these records might be found. This would have opened up another whole resource area had I needed to go this route.

Summer over, another season, another burst of searching. It was time to put more emphasis on using the few items of information I had about my mother, time to pick up the thread of her university background. I read and reread the sentence "She completed high school, went on to graduate and then to work at her profession" and became even more convinced that I must search post-secondary school institutions. At first I thought that it might be possible to go through the Ontario Department of Education for records of those who had a high school leaving certificate, but these are not kept in any one central register, so I moved on to university records. I didn't go back as far as high school records at this point since they would inevitably involve a greater number of institutions and longer lists of names. If the university records came up with a blank I could try high schools. The alumni offices of the universities of Guelph, Toronto, Western, and Queen's did searches of their alumni through the years in which she might have graduated. I realized from this search just how few Attwoods graduated from university, and although for some time there was no record of a female Attwood with my mother's biographical details, it did give me hope, because it proved once again that I was dealing with an uncommon name, which would be easier to track down when it appeared, and I felt that she had to appear *somewhere*. Just as I was giving up hope, the alumni office of the University of Toronto informed me that they had a record of a girl from Ottawa who had been born in 1912 and who graduated in 1932. They would give me no information as to her whereabouts except to say that she had moved to Winnipeg. Could this be the one I had been praying for? This information tied in not only with the approximate dates of my mother's birth, but also with the clue of their moving west. The woman in the alumni office offered to forward a letter to her.

On October 10, 1984 I sent the following letter:

I am writing to you courtesy of the University of Toronto Alumni office who have agreed to send this letter on. I am searching for a relative, and in this search am contacting Attwoods wherever I can find them, university graduation records being one source.

It is very difficult tracing people by their maiden name, especially when one does not have a first name but only biographical details. I am hoping the facts which I will now relate may be those of someone in your branch of the Attwood family.

The lady whom I am trying to contact was born in 1912 or 1913. Her parents were born in England and immigrated to Canada where she and her three elder sisters and one brother were born. The sisters married, but I have no information as to whether her brother married or not. She married an Englishman who came to Canada in the 1920s after seeing service in the British armed services in the First War and I believe he served in the

Canadian forces during the Second War. This was a second marriage for him, and I believe that he was some years older than she and was in his forties when he married again.

I realize that this is an unusual request, and I thank you for your time. Any assistance, or further leads will be most gratefully appreciated.

Just twelve days later she wrote back from British Columbia:

I'm sorry that I can be of no help. Our branch of the Attwoods came to Canada just after the Battle of Waterloo and have had no contact with any English branch, as far as I know. In fact, I have never run into any other Attwoods spelt with 2 Ts. I hope you succeed in your search.

I was becoming discouraged, for I did not know where else to turn to find this elusive female Attwood. I had already eliminated the other possibility — that it might be my father's surname — when I had checked with the military archives and drawn a blank. I didn't even want to consider the third possibility: that my name might have been chosen more or less at random. I'm afraid that does happen in some cases.

I was discouraged, but nowhere near ready to give up. Academic records, I thought, might be the best area to tackle next. Every child goes to school, so my birth mother's files had to be *somewhere*! Conceivably she had been educated out of province, and I was prepared to contact every university in North America. That was a long shot, though, and I put it on the back burner as a possible last-ditch effort. I called a doctor friend in Montreal to find out what the rights of an individual are with regard to medical files. After my earlier experience of being rebuffed by authorities, it was easier to call sympathetic friends whom I could trust for facts. You never know what ulterior motive someone may have for not giving you factual information, or they may just be ignorant. One becomes quite distrusting after having doors slammed in one's face at regular intervals. My friend told me that an individual has the right to his or her full dossier. I wrote back to the hospital where I was born asking for more information, and in time received a letter back saying that the birth and weight charts were all that I had, and that they could not release my mother's chart.

About this time I read Betty Jean Lifton's touching book *Lost and Found*. She identified five stages in the process of searching for and making contact with the birth family. It was helpful, because it provided more evidence that my feelings were "normal." She defines the stages thus:

1. *Threshold:*
   "The search requires not only courage but cunning and persistence. . . . Even the most law-abiding adoptee, who is mortified by a traffic violation, soon finds himself sneaking about surreptitiously for information, often lying and impersonating others to achieve his goals."

2. *Obsession:*
   ". . . the search becomes an obsession. . . . A game

to be played for its own sake. . . . Adoptees become obsessed with piecing together the puzzle, finding the missing parts. . . . They need this period to gather psychic strength for the moment they will penetrate the veil."

3. *Limbo:*
   "The state of being where one has some information and yet hesitates to contact the birth mother or anyone in the family who may have information as to her whereabouts."

4. *Fantasy:*
   "Fantasy and fear make up the landscape of Limbo Land." [This is the time wondering what "they" (the birth family) are *really* like.]

5. *Penetrating the Veil:*
   [The adoptee] "musters up the psychic energy to make contact between the past and the present, the living and the dead. One part of them is still terrified, but the other part drives determinedly on."

I found that, for me, *obsession, limbo* and *fantasy* overlapped in time, but it is certainly well to be forewarned of what can happen. Stage three is at its most powerful when you wonder whether you are doing the right thing. The temptation at this stage is to sit back and do nothing or to run frantically in small circles. If you are truly determined, it will pass!

So. It was back to the newspapers for death notices.

Maybe, just maybe, my father's death would have been noted. I didn't know his name, but maybe there would be something about "Mourned by his loving wife — X Attwood." It took an hour and a half to read the files for one month and I soon realized that this was a ridiculous, time-wasting tack. There are times when one has to admit a brilliant idea is really not so brilliant after all, and is really just a sop to your frustration and need to be doing something. This is when you are truly in limbo.

I thrashed around for several days at this point feeling frustrated, angry, helpless and generally despondent about the whole search. I was still reading anything and everything I could get my hands on about adoption searches, comforting myself with the stories of others out there who were feeling as I felt, and with the knowledge that we were a significant group in society, whose needs and psyches were being investigated by researchers. This is the period of your research when you need all the support your family can give you but must remember that *it isn't their search*. Unless your significant other was also adopted, he or she isn't really going to understand. It is the ghost in *your* life, you own it, nobody else. If they sometimes seem uncomprehending, or unable to grasp why you are so obsessively driven to search, accept with grateful thanks the understanding that they *do* give, no matter how little or how much. Love, understanding, information — take what you can get!

In frustration I phoned my cousin, who had given me so much information and support, and pleaded, "What more can you tell me? You must know more!" I had learned an interesting thing about telephone conversations. As time passes, people begin to remember more. I

was patient, forgot about the phone bill and let the tide
of words ebb and flow. Invariably, *something* comes of
each contact.

This time my cousin, who had been a legal secretary,
told me something that I had never known, and which I
don't think I have heard anywhere else. Wills are in the
public domain. You can write to the surrogate court in
the provincial capital for anybody's will since 1945 and
it will be sent to you. They seal adoption records, but the
disposal of a person's whole life savings and possessions
to their nearest and dearest is visible for everyone!

I was back into action. I went over all the names I had
gleaned, and sent off for the wills of those that I knew
had died. Reading them gave me a greater feeling of
invasion of privacy than anything I did during my whole
search. The purpose of this tack was to add more people
to my family trees, more people to get in touch with. Of
course, I was also hoping that one of the people for whom
I was searching might have been a beneficiary. Nothing
came of this, but it might have!

My small card birth certificate, which was all that I
could ever obtain, had my birth date wrong, and I had
never bothered to get it changed. According to it, I was
two weeks younger than I actually was. It now seemed
to me that a request to get it corrected was a perfect ploy
to see whether I could get a copy of my long form.
Non-adopted persons can request a copy of their full
birth certificate, known as the long form, which gives
place of birth and parents' full names. I sent off a formal,
typewritten letter enclosing my old card, pointing out
the error and requesting a new card. I also asked for it to
be corrected on my original certificate, and asked for

copies to be sent to me so that I could verify that it had been done. Maybe, just maybe, the clerk handling it would not be paying attention and send me both. Stories have been told of adoptees receiving their long form under such circumstances. I learned to write at the beginning of the week so that my request would arrive during the mid-week rush when the staff might be too busy to notice. (Another school of thought suggests writing at the end of the week so your letter will be buried in the Monday morning pile when the clerks are still recovering from the weekend!)

No luck. The short certificate came back, with the correction, but with no mention of my request for copies. I sent a second letter saying basically the same thing, but signed it with my birth name. No reply. There are tales of adoptees who have asked for their birth certificate, signing the letter with their birth name, and the clerk for whatever reason — because she was sympathetic, or because she was interrupted, or she wanted to get the last letter out before quitting time on a Friday — did send the original copy. Also worth a try.

Rereading the non-identifying information and my sources list, it struck me again that I had been with my birth parents for two weeks after my birth. They had named me, and perhaps they had had me baptized. If they had, my name and those of my parents would be listed in church records somewhere. But where? What church? Another letter to the Children's Aid, this time asking them if there was any mention of information relating to baptism. Somewhere I had read that often there is information in these files that counts as non-identifying, but which the social worker doesn't think is particularly significant, and so does not include in the information that is sent to you. It is worth asking questions after receipt of the non-identifying information. All it takes is one more letter and a stamp!

My father had been stationed in Barrie, and I was born there, so it seemed that would be a logical place to start my investigation of church records. Our parish priest gave me the name of the minister of the Anglican church which had, in fact, been the garrison church during the time my father had been posted there.

The feeling of excitement that one has while following up a long-shot lead grows out of all proportion to its real possibilities. Emotions go up and down like a roller coaster, and the smallest hopeful sign can result in almost childlike excitement. The minister was helpful, interested and understanding. I told him the truth about my search and he promised to check their records. This kind gentleman, without any suggestion on my part, contacted as well the other churches in the town and asked their ministers and priests to check their files. Two weeks later he called back with disappointing news. There was no record of any Attwood membership or baptism. The roller coaster slid downward. A small donation was my only way of showing my deep appreciation.

My father had been a patient in the sanatorium in Gravenhurst, or at least I had hearsay evidence to that effect. I called the Muskoka Centre (as it is now called) for their patient records. No one seemed to know what had happened to them. How could years and years of the records of a major medical centre simply disappear? Had they really, or was someone just to busy to care? Another item relegated to the "to do if desperate" page.

November brought long winter evenings and the first snows of the season. It was time for another trip to Toronto, and more time in the Ontario Archives. I devoted this period to searching the probate indexes looking for other Attwoods whom I had perhaps missed in my other searches. I found that there was another clutch of the family in Walkerton. Taking advantage of the time I had, I went through all the Ontario telephone directories, cross-checking them with the city directories that were available, this time looking for maternal grandparents. I found enough Attwoods in the Walkerton phone books to make it worth a trip.

Accompanied by my friend of the late nights, I headed off through the snowy western Ontario countryside. Our first stop was at the town hall offices of Heritage Walkerton. The archivist, a gentle, bearded young man, regaled us with stories of the early days of the town, stories of immigration, settlement, and pioneer hardship. He offered, for an extremely small fee, to do a newspaper search on the Attwoods. He then dug out the cemetery records and we searched for the location of the family graves. It was certainly far more comfortable doing this general search inside a warm office, but eventually we had to go out and brave the elements. We left the town and drove along concession roads to the cemetery, which was tucked quietly away in the corner of a field. It was a bitterly cold, windy day — just the sort of day one associates with visits to graveyards.

We first drove and then walked up and down the aisles of stones that silently marked generations long gone. Comparing dates, we rapidly came to the conclusion that none of these people were significant to the search. Returning to the office, we went through the references to the family that the archivist had found while we were gone. They had done some interesting things, these Walkerton Attwoods; we read of their marriages and deaths recorded in Victorian small-town prose for posterity. However, they were to remain in my files only as souvenirs of the search. A great number of Walkerton people had gone west to Manitoba. I knew that my family had gone out west (hearsay again). Could they have done so to be near family? Another item for the "when desperate" file.

Back in Toronto, I returned to the Ontario Archives and started reading land grant and cemetery archives. Long on interest, short on facts. I decided to go back to the telephone books. This time I made a list of all the Attwoods in all the phone books in Ontario in the 1940s. I had laid an honest claim to my microfiche machine by this time! On returning home, I sent the list to all the contacts I had made and asked them to identify anyone they could. Again, everyone responded, but nothing useful or positive for my long-term goal was established.

Following the lead that my maternal grandparents might have lived in Toronto, I wrote to city hall for assessment records. This was the only official organization that never replied. Had it been necessary, they would have got a second request by registered mail.

One of the most frustrating things at this point was that I was still not one-hundred-percent sure that Attwood was my mother's name. All the evidence pointed to it, since my father was not listed in the National Defence Archives under Attwood, but there was still nothing to link it to my mother after all this time. Surely something should have surfaced.

It was time to go back to trying to find more information about my father. I widened my inquiries and wrote to National Defence Archives in England; after all, he had been in the British forces during the First World War. Some cross-checking was in order. Some time later, a letter arrived stating that there was no record of any such Attwood — but that many of their files had been destroyed during the Blitz.

At the end of November a letter came from Children's Aid stating that my mother was Anglican and my father had no stated religion. Another lead, and proof that there was more information that could be classified as non-identifying sitting in my file. If I couldn't find out about my baptism, then I would see if I could find out where my mother had been baptized. All I knew was that she came from a small town in Ontario, so I wrote to the Archives of the Anglican church to find out how their baptismal records were organized for the early years of the century. The reply came back promptly at the beginning of December saying that they would need more information before they could search. They did, however, enclose the addresses of all the diocesan offices in Canada. I knew how they felt: I was stymied myself without more information. If all the records had been in one place, I would willingly have gone through them, page by page, parish by parish. I did write to each diocese in Canada to find how their records were organized, just in case it did become necessary to broaden my search.

The problem with church records is that you need to know the area from which the family came. As the sec-

retary of the Diocese of Algoma pointed out, their diocese covers 70,000 square miles, from Bracebridge in the
south to Englehart in the north, and from Témiscaming,
in the east to Thunder Bay in the west. She did indicate
a willingness to search registers for an area, and went on
to say that if she was not successful, or if registers were
missing, she would give me the names and addresses of
clergymen in the area. The Diocese of Keewatin did do a
search of their registers. The records of the Diocese of
Huron are kept in the V.P. Cronyn Memorial Archives at
Huron College in London, Ont. The Diocese Archives of
Toronto has on deposit many parish registers from
churches within the diocese, but they are not indexed or
microfilmed. A search for a family in this area involves
going through the original volumes on the basis of dates
and any location of residence that you may have. Church
records are a long shot, but they certainly are a source
well worth tapping.

An interesting letter came in at this point from a gentleman I had forgotten I had even written to several
months before — an Attwood in Barrie. He wrote to say
that he was related to the Glace Bay Attwoods.

Another connection that had been left hanging for
almost a year was the original "Y" Attwood, the secretary
who had married the "Z" Bailey who worked in an
insurance office. The birth announcement of their child
was in the Toronto paper, but then they had disappeared
from the Toronto directories in the late forties, only to
reappear in the sixties. So much of this fitted, how had I
ever lost this clue? A letter from my London contact put
me in touch with a distant relative of his who was "Y's"
sister. From her biographical details it was clear it was

the wrong family, though it had looked so promising for so long. Disappointment. But more names for the family tree.

At this same time a letter from the Queen's University Archives told me of a Charles H. Attwood in Manitoba. My last act for the year was to write to the Manitoba Archives.

Another whole year had gone by and I really was no further ahead. I began asking myself how much more time I was willing to put into this. It wasn't a question of becoming bored with the project, far from it; but I had to be realistic — didn't I? However, there were so many dangling ends that I knew that I couldn't leave it just yet.

7

BREAKTHROUGH!

Adoption was originally considered one incident in a person's life. It is now realized and accepted that adoption is an ongoing process in which the individual must cope and adjust throughout his/her life.

Lynn Giddens, *Faces of Adoption*

M EMORIES, GIVEN TIME, surface like rocks in a spring field. My search had stirred up some interesting developments in my London contact's family. He had become more interested in his ancestry as a result of my questions and had discovered from his elderly father that there had been six in his father's family, not two as he had always thought. Could one of these "lost" brothers be my maternal grandfather? He also remembered a military man in the lodge who had worked, he thought, with London Life. He put me in touch with a retired amateur archivist who had been doing research into the history of both his old firm, London Life, and his lodge. What more could one ask? This delightful gentleman, who was to become my most significant and long-standing supporter, asked me to write down everything, "including what your father liked for breakfast, if you know," and send it to him. I kept in regular touch with him and am eternally grateful for his encouragement and help, all freely given just for the excitement of the chase. It was information I received from him that, by the process of elimination, finally led me to the successful conclusion of my search. I have yet to meet him, but someday we will go to lunch.

My letters began to bear fruit. A response came in from another Attwood who was one of nine sisters. More names that could be eliminated from family trees.

In February, 1985, I widened my search to the Hamilton area, where I had an old friend from my university days. I hesitated to call her, for our relationship had dwindled over the past twenty years to the Christmas-card letter stage, but if you can't call on old friends, who can you call on? I telephoned her, we chatted for a few minutes about this and that, and then I proceeded to tell her the real reason for my call. She was fascinated about my quest, for she had not known I was adopted, and readily agreed to let her fingers do the walking through Hamilton and district telephone books. She phoned me the next night with a list of seven Attwoods. I called these numbers, and again went into my story about genealogical research. They were all most co-operative, but only two of them tied into family trees that I had on file. The other five helped me develop new trees, but no new leads resulted. One of the families had only been in Canada for seven years. They told me that there were large numbers of Attwoods in the Coventry and Liverpool areas in

England. If I had to go back a generation to England, that would certainly tie into two locations that had suffered severe bombing. I thought Coventry would be the obvious city to start with in any attempt to trace my grandmother's death, for it was famous for one extremely heavy raid, whereas Liverpool had suffered numerous times. There had to be an easier way, but I was prepared to take my search to England if necessary.

I was beginning to wonder if there could have been an error in the non-identifying information in the matter of the size of my mother's family. The name was not that common; surely I must have touched on all the families by now. Not one of the families I had tracked down had four girls and one boy. I decided to call Children's Aid yet again to ask them to confirm the size of my birth mother's family. This fragment of information, the basis of so many of my inquiries, *had* to be correct. I took a chance and asked them if they could tell me which of my parents was the Attwood. This certainly would have been identifying information, but I hoped that maybe, just maybe, the social worker would tell me, considering that I had discovered a name. Maybe persistence would pay off and earn me some pity. The social worker promised to check my files again for size of the family but told me curtly that my other question strayed into the realm of identifying information.

In the midst of all this a letter arrived from the Manitoba archives identifying Charles Attwood as a government official of some note. I wrote back asking for biographical details of his family.

A letter from my archivist-insurance agent-lodge brother arrived in almost the same mail saying that he had had no luck whatsoever in his inquiries. He had gone to great lengths to dredge up information. "I phoned London Life and they do not keep records after seven years. Yesterday two of us looked through our records going back to before the 1920s but saw no Attwood name except that of J. who is a member of the lodge, as you know. From 1920 to 1950 we only had about two Attwoods in the city directory." He went on to tell me that he had tracked one of these down to an address, and had gone to speak to a neighbour, who remembered him but said that Mr. Attwood had died a number of years before. "I have gone through hundreds of minutes and have seen the names of the men who joined up but never have seen an Attwood name, if I had, I would have told J." He concluded, "If you do have any other ideas, be sure to let me know if I can help you as I do enjoy this research."

In April I received another letter from him with this delightful opening line: "What is this power you have over men, why do they JUMP when you ask them to do something! I phoned the school board and they said they have lists of students and I said that I would be glad to go to help. DO NOT GIVE UP YET, I will do as you command." I had a good chuckle over this letter, for I have never figured charisma to be one of my strong points!

This was the beginning of another dark time in my search. Nothing! Strong leads went nowhere. Every contact was negative. The only thing I had done was to build up family trees and discover a great deal of interesting material about families that were not mine. I spent hours going over my notes. What had I missed? Was there something so obvious that it couldn't be seen? Was I so involved that I was going about the whole thing the wrong way?

A great deal has been written recently about lateral thinking, so I deliberately tried to look at the whole mess from different angles. The only concrete information I had discovered was contained in a list of names, and the relationships and inter-relationships of people from four seemingly unrelated families. If my mother had been an only child it was conceivable that I could have missed her, but with three sisters and a brother they had to be somewhere. Should I broaden my search outside Ontario? I couldn't face that at this stage, and besides, something told me that they were here.

What use was all this? Was it really worth the time and the effort? Friends and family kindly listened to my thoughts over and over. Several times I put the whole matter away, determined to forget about it and let it rest, only to pull all my notes out a few hours later. I found difficulty in concentrating on anything for any great length of time, my mind kept returning to the search, to the fantasy of what I would say to my mother when I found her, to what I would say if I "tripped" over a relative, to what I would do if years continued to go by like this. How long was I willing to keep it up?

Then it hit me. I had been looking for names *on* the family tree and trying to add more and more, but *elimination* was the key. I knew my birth mother was born in 1911 or 1912. I knew several other women who shared the surname on the family trees of the same generation. How many Attwood females could be born in Ontario in 1911 or 1912? Logic says not many. If I could get the Ontario birth records of 1911 and 1912, they would tell me the actual names of the Attwood females born in those years. Several names then could be struck off this list since I knew they were not from my birth family. Thus, it followed that one of the remaining names would be my mother. Then it would be simply (what an easy word!) a case of tracking down each of the remaining names, finding out who they married and where they were now! Convoluted thinking, but it made sense. My hobby of doing British logic problems was paying off.

It would be a massive job, but my inquiries would then be based on known names, not on biographical details. Why hadn't I thought of it before? Though even if I had, I still would have needed the time to build up the family trees, so that the list of names left wouldn't be so large.

Fortunately, another trip to Toronto was on the agenda the week after this illumination. Leaving home a couple of days early I rolled down the 401 and made my way to the Registrar General's Office, a never to be forgotten place. My problems started with the quest for a parking place. That half hour spent driving around and around the block past parking lots with "Full" signs was almost unbearable. When at last someone pulled out right in front of the building, I had to resist the temptation to flag the driver down and thank him. Joggle into the tight slot, lock the doors, feed the meter, pass security, go up the escalator, proceed down an endless hallway to the wrong offices, retrace steps, turn down another long hall, and finally, pass through the great wooden doors at the end. No quiet office this — the place was wall-to-wall humanity. Dutifully taking a number, which was about twenty from the head of the line, I sat down to wait. Babies were being registered, marriages were being recorded for posterity, an Eastern gentleman who had never had a Canadian passport was trying to confirm his citizenship for an emergency passport to return home for a funeral. Endless conversations as the line crept forward. At last, my number was called. A kindly middle-aged woman sat ensconced behind her computer screen.

"Yes?"

"I would like to obtain a list of all the female Attwoods born in 1911 and 1912."

"I beg your pardon?" She lifted her eyebrows; apparently my request was an unusual one, and the poor soul seemed quite taken aback. I repeated myself.

"I'm sorry, I can't give you that information."

"But aren't birth records open to the public?"

"I'm sorry."

Here was a case where she had the facts and I didn't. Was she right or was she lazy? Or didn't she know how to cope with a question she hadn't heard before? Maybe she figured that the safest way out was to simply refuse to give me the information.

"There is no way?"

"No, I'm sorry." Her gaze moved over my shoulder to the individual behind me and I, and my problem, were dismissed.

I turned and made my way dejectedly past the lines of waiting humanity and out through the great heavy doors and back down the endless corridor. I was *so sure* that there would be no problem in getting a simple list of those born in a certain year. Once again my hopes were completely dashed. I felt beaten. What harm could come from knowing who was born in Ontario in a certain year? I had been flipping through so many old files, discovering so much information that this seemed entirely innoc-uous, bordering on deadly dull. Yet for some reason the facts were not available. This was carrying sealed records too far!

The escalator bore me to the doors and I stepped out into the cold wind sweeping off the lake. Sheer frustra-tion swept over me. Everything seemed futile. I had long since stopped thinking about the file that was sitting in the Ontario Social Services Archives with my name on it, which could so easily have solved everything.

Reluctant to give up my parking space I went into a seedy little restaurant that boasted nothing more than a blaring jukebox and a half-dozen small, grungy tables. Dropping into a chair and ordering a coffee from a surprisingly friendly waitress, I pulled my papers from my briefcase and spread them out in front of me. I had studied these notes so often I knew them by heart, but lurking somewhere in those dog-eared, scrawled pages was one fact, one concept, one link that would clear up the problem. *A had married B, they had six children, one had been killed in the North Atlantic. That was the University of Toronto grad's uncle; another had moved to the States* . . . and on and on. I had conclusively eliminated each of them as a possible relative. Another cup of dreadful coffee. Did I want to risk lunch? No, definitely not.

There had to be a key. Why couldn't I see it? Another coffee that I really didn't want. What I did want was the table and a warm place to think. The cost was reasonable under the circumstances, and the place would be toler-able if I could just do something about the joker who kept feeding coins into the jukebox. I took out a fresh piece of paper and wrote down the names of all the women who had been of my birth mother's generation, even the ones I had definitely eliminated — these I marked with a star. I stared at them, willing them to tell me what to do. What if I was to take these names back to the Registrar General's guardian? I had asked her to give me names, but if I had the names and asked her for facts about them, would that shed a different light on things? It was worth a shot. I shuffled everything back into my briefcase, put the list of names into my purse, paid the bill and set out once again to do battle. Past my parking meter, feeding it the maximum amount en route, up the escalator, down the right hallway, through the wooden doors, another number far, far down the list. The lady I had spoken to glanced up with a slight expression of surprise as she spotted me sitting in the rows in front of her. The line moved slowly and I let a couple of people go ahead of me so I could speak to her again.

"Could you tell me how *many* Attwood females you have on your list who were born in 1911 or 1912?" No way could that be confidential information. She looked mildly puzzled.

She thought for a moment — this was beyond her list of well-rehearsed answers — then she relented. "Well, yes, I guess I could do that." She addressed herself to her computer keyboard. *Clickity clickity,* encouraging hums. "There are two born in 1911, none in 1912." This was better than I could possibly have wished for.

I took out my list of the seven names of Attwood females born during the first twenty years of the century, and pushed it across the desk towards her. "Can you tell me if those two names are here on this list?"

What justification could she have for refusing? She

would not be giving out any specific or identifying information. She read the names and then looked up at her computer screen. Yes, she said, both names were on my list, and she ticked them off. I took the paper, and my worst fears were realized. She had ticked the two names I had starred.

Sitting in the car, I let the implications of what I had just learned sink in. There had only been two born in those years, and since those two had already been eliminated (one was one of the nine sisters, and the other was my London contact's cousin) *Attwood could not be my mother's name!* The other five were flotsam and jetsam — they were either too old or too young to be my birth mother. I had eliminated Attwood four years before as my father's name with the very first phone call of my search, because I knew he had been in the Canadian army and there was no Attwood registered. Tears of frustration flowed down my cheeks for the first time. Something was terribly, terribly wrong. Had I wasted four years chasing false names? Was there something radically wrong with my non-identifying information? I was devastated.

However, I had to leave to go to London where I had interviews the next day. Pulling out into the rush hour traffic, I spent the next hour on the Gardiner Expressway, working my way out to the Q.E.W. in a traditional Toronto traffic jam. I didn't need the snowstorm that was adding its bleakness to my mood.

I was staying with an old, old friend, a girl I had grown up with but had not seen for over ten years. The first thing I did on reaching her home was to call J.A.R. (my helpful London contact) and check the birth date of his cousin. It was right. How I wished I had made a mistake!

Over dinner I told Gail and her husband of my search and my dilemma; I was surprised when she reacted with "You never told me you were adopted." There really was a time in my life when it wasn't important! They were fascinated and wanted to help. It was another night of brainstorming into the wee, wee hours. Her husband was a "London boy," who thought that maybe some of his old contacts might know another "old London family," who had had a divorce way back when. Divorces were not common in the 1940s and were likely to have been remembered. He would do some surreptitious inquiring.

After my interview with the prospective staff member at the university, I went to the library to try telephone books and cemetery archives, although at this point I don't know what I was looking for, other than following up insurance company leads. London is the centre of the Ontario insurance industry so I took advantage of the chance to look through some old records. Did I really expect to turn a page and see my father's name staring out at me? It is amazing how much time one can waste in aimless thrashing, just to satisfy the need to be doing something. The day was essentially wasted. I had meant to call Mr. K, my helpful amateur archivist friend, for this would have been a perfect time to invite him to lunch and put a face to the handwriting and friendly voice. But I was so discouraged that I couldn't summon the energy to even make a telephone call. I had always considered "I don't want to talk about it" to be the ultimate cop-out. Now I knew how people who used that expression felt. I made work for myself until mid-afternoon, when I could safely consider the worst of the rush hour on the 401 to be over, and headed back to Toronto.

I was almost frantic. The next morning I decided to storm the bastions of the Children's Aid Society one more time and demand some answers. Parking illegally (this was no time for niceties), I charged up the stairs and asked to see the social worker I had been corresponding with over the years. She had retired!

The receptionist took me to a sparse, bare, tiny room. A desk huddled beside a grimy window overlooking a parking lot. Leafless trees stood defiant of the city around them. Everything was plain, bleak and drab, matching my spirit.

A young woman entered. "May I help you?" she asked pleasantly. If only she could! I briefly recounted my story and my dilemma. "Something has to be wrong," I concluded helplessly. I told her I knew, and understood, that she could not give me any specific details. All I needed to know was if the facts on my non-identifying information sheet were correct. Typing errors did occur and if one number was wrong relating to my mother's age, then that would explain one part of the problem and I could start again with the five names that were left. Sympathetically, I thought, she agreed to check my file once more and let me know by mail. At least there was no lecture, no questioning of my motives. Why should I expect there to be? The guilt of the adoptee is never far below the surface.

Three weeks later, this letter arrived:

Following your visit, I followed up on your question, that being of your father's legal name and your mother's number of siblings and her birth date. The information you received in 1982 and 1984 was correct. All other information cannot be confirmed or denied as this constitutes identifying information.

The next months passed in questioning, rereading and re-evaluating the information I had scraped up over four long years. I could see no flaw in my reasoning or in my search, except perhaps all the useless trails I had followed, but that was inevitable.

With the coming of spring, I called Children's Aid once more and spoke to the same young social worker. I had to try again. Maybe this time! They were the only known, concrete link that I had to my past. Maybe some interfering social worker had picked a name that had nothing to do with my parents and had put that on the birth certificate. There were records of that having been done, and there were so many games played with the original birth certificates that anything was possible. I decided to ask.

"Was my name a 'John Doe' name, picked for convenience and anonymity from the phone book?" It was essentially the same question I had asked during my visit, which the letters had answered, but . . .

Pause . . .

"No, your name was the name of one of your birth parents."

"Which one?"

Pause . . .

"I'm sorry, that would be identifying information, which I can't give you."

What else did I expect? I didn't know what to say, and surprisingly for me said nothing at all, but just let the silence hang as the long distance charges ticked away. Much to my surprise she spoke again:

"But I can tell you if you are wrong — if you ask me."
My heart stopped. This was it! I had finally, through
sheer perseverance, gotten through. She had taken pity
on me. The answer was only a word or two away.
"Was it my mother's name?"
"No."
"Then it was my father's!"
"I didn't tell you that."
The answer! Four years, seven years, all my life now I
knew my father had given me his name. A simple thank
you seemed too insignificant, there were no words that
could possibly express my gratitude. I wired a bouquet
of flowers to that wonderful social worker with a heart.
I hope that by now enough time has passed that it will
be impossible to identify her and that there will be no
repercussions for her. Someone was human, someone
could not cope with the hypocrisy.

I had a name. A real name. A real father. But why hadn't
my very first phone call four years before to the archives
of the Ministry of Defence told me that? I had asked them
to check for an Attwood in the Canadian forces, and my
father *had* been in the forces, that was a fact I knew beyond
a doubt. I went back to my notes and to my files. They had
very clearly stated that there was no Attwood with the
biographical details of my father. Children's Aid had confirmed that that information had been correct. What had
gone wrong? There was no point torturing myself with
unanswerable questions, I simply had to start the search
all over again to trace Attwood as my father.

I called my cousin in Guelph to give her an update and
to confirm that the time when she had been with my
parents was between the spring of 1945 and July 1948. I

no longer trusted *any* of the information I had so painstakingly collected. From now on I would double-check
everything and never again risk going off half-cocked on
a search with false pieces of information. With these
dates firmly established I felt confident that my mother
must have seen the birth announcement of my brother
or sister during this time period. She had seen it, there
were microfilms, so somehow I would find it. Back to
newspaper archives I went, to check birth announcements from 1945 to 1949. Now I knew what name I was
looking for — but hadn't I done this all before? Why
hadn't I found it? I checked my files to make sure that I
wasn't repeating myself. Had I missed a month here or
there? Had some file been missing from the library, or at
someone else's desk when I wanted it, and had I forgotten to go back to it? Where were my mistakes, my missing
spots? I wasted a lot of time at this point, for like a
lemming rushing unthinkingly to the cliff I plunged into
activity just to be doing something, anything.

A note in my book tells me that I wrote to the Registrar
General for death certificates of male Attwoods between
1960 and 1964. Nothing seems to have come of this,
which is strange, as my father died in 1964. Perhaps
death certificates, like marriage certificates, are not available to the casual inquirer. I failed to complete my notes
on this. I didn't need to write for his will, but that would
have been the next step, and I would likely have been
able to find the names of his beneficiaries. Things started
to happen fairly quickly at that point, and my record-
keeping became somewhat sloppy. However, once the
truth is known, there is no further need to keep track of
clues.

A visit to the Sherbrooke Department of Immigration to inquire about getting immigration records (my birth father had immigrated to Canada in the 1920s) left me feeling that this would be an extremely time-consuming approach. Immigration records are stored all over the country and under many different classifications. It is possible to read the lists of passengers on ships, but it is necessary to contact the shipping lines for their records. Landed-immigrant records are available, but in the period just after the First World War there were thousands of immigrants coming to Canada. Going through citizenship records would be another possibility, but many people, especially those from Britain, did not take out Canadian citizenship for some time, if ever, after their initial entry to the country. I did write to the Department of Employment and Immigration in Ottawa requesting information on the immigration to Canada of the Attwood family. However, without specific information as to dates they were unable to do a search of their records. They did say that if I could travel to the Ottawa-Hull area, arrangements could be made for me to visit the office personally to view their records.

I could have gone mad during this period if I had let myself dwell on the years I had wasted tracing my mother and her family with a name that was my father's. Essentially, four years were totally wasted, except that I had compiled the information that finally forced me to eliminate Attwood as her name and drove me to my final impassioned plea to Children's Aid. Positive results from futile efforts.

I could think of only two more things to do. First, to go back to telephone directories, for I hadn't kept records of the names and phone numbers once they had, as I thought, outlived their usefulness. A classic demonstration of the wisdom of keeping everything. It might be useful again, even though you cannot see how. Second, to write yet again to all my original contacts with a revised set of data — I was looking for a man, not a woman.

I felt very discouraged at having to do all this again, and a little awkward at having to contact people again. However, I didn't really care what they thought; there had been enough lies and deception that a little more confusion wouldn't really make much difference — and I would never meet them anyway. The only exceptions were those I had written to early in my search, before I had the information from the military archives. I had said in those letters that I wasn't sure whether I was looking for a male or a female and had given them both sets of information. I decided that before writing to anyone again I could go to the head office of Bell Canada in Montreal and tackle the telephone books.

Leaving my car on Beaver Hall Hill I started to search, surfacing each hour to feed the parking meter. I went back to the Toronto books for 1942, 1969, and 1971 to see who had appeared, disappeared (to correlate with the hearsay evidence that my parents had moved out west) and reappeared (the hearsay that they had come back to Ontario), and then disappeared (the death of my father). This was the first time that I had done an in-depth search actually trying to follow the movement of individuals by use of telephone books. The only connection I had with Toronto was that elusive birth announcement. I then moved on to small-town Ontario and made a list of all

Attwoods living in Ontario. Mrs. Attwood, if she was
still alive, had to be one of those names. Four hours
later I emerged from the Bell offices with a new list of
Attwoods. Six inches of wet, soggy April snow covered the concrete, rush hour traffic slipped and
slithered and I still had a two-hour drive ahead of me.
It was not until I was halfway across the Champlain
Bridge, windshield wipers barely coping with the
slush, that I noticed the piece of paper stuck to the
corner of my windshield. A parking ticket. What a
souvenir!

The next day was the first of May, and a new beginning.
I set to work to track down the error. It had to be in the
military archives. The first thing I did was to call the
ever-patient Francine and ask her to check the files one
more time. Several times in my search I had had problems with the one and two "t" spellings. Could that have
been the error that caused the problem? My first query
had been written (I checked my copy, I had not made a
spelling error), but my further contacts had been oral.
She said she would check and call me back.

A few hours later the phone rang, and it was Francine.
"I think I may have found something. We have a William,
who was born in 1901, and an Ernest born in 1900. It will
take a few days to find out the biographical details, but
I'll get back to you at the beginning of the week. I do hope
this is it."

That was one of the longest weekends I have ever
spent. I kept myself occupied by going through the
Toronto Star microfilms, which had arrived on inter-library loan, searching for that elusive birth announce-

ment. Another blank, but it didn't really matter now. I was just keeping busy.

True to her word, Francine called Monday at midday. "I think I have good news for you. We have a Captain Walter Ernest Attwood, file number 430904. He was born in England in 1900 and died February 14, 1964. There is a record of a divorce on file. Is that the man you have been looking for?"

Francine's calm, familiar voice on the telephone from two hundred miles away was giving me the news that I had spent years waiting, searching, and hoping for. I couldn't believe I was actually hearing his name. Walter. Wally.

"Yes, oh, yes, Francine! You've found my father!"

Even over the long-distance telephone line I knew she had a sense of success, and of joy in my joy.

"Why couldn't the person I spoke to four years ago have told me that?" I asked.

She sighed. "The only thing I can think of is that they just checked Attwood with two 't's. I checked that again and it wasn't there, but you were so sure that I decided to try Atwood with one 't,' and there he was. His name is spelled right, that is, with two 't's, but it was just filed in the wrong place. I'm so sorry, I should have thought of that a long time ago."

I couldn't believe it! Some stupid, inefficient, careless clerk had robbed me of four years of my life in a fruitless search!

Francine sounded as if she thought she was responsible, poor girl. I spent several minutes reassuring her that it certainly wasn't her fault, thanked her again, and hung up with the new-found name ringing in my ears.

A filing error!

The time had not been entirely wasted. It gave me a frustrating but vital interval of contemplation. At the beginning I had not been absolutely sure of the rightness of what I was doing, but during those four years I had gathered enough proof to have a secure sense that the family would accept my contacting them. And I had had time to cope with my own emotions, as bit by bit I delved deeper and deeper into my past.

It was now just a matter of going back to my list from the Ontario phone books and looking for W.E. Had my birth mother left the phone listing in my father's name? If it wasn't there, I would have contacted them all. Now I had a name, and it would only be a matter of time.

8

CONTACT

> *Genealogical connection is one important*
> *aspect of adult identity, relating each*
> *individual to past and future generations.*
> *Adoption, by its very nature, severs this*
> *connection, leaving a void and a sense of*
> *biological rootlessness. Lack of knowledge*
> *and sense of one's true identity cannot be*
> *overcome, no matter how warm and*
> *nurturing adoptive parents are.*
> A.D. Sorosky et al., *The Adoption Triangle:*
> *The Effect of Sealed Records*

O PENING MY NOTEBOOK to the last entries I had made
at the telephone offices, I ran my finger down the
list, *and there it was*, part-way down page two. W.E.
Attwood, XXX Y Ave., Small Town, Ont. She was alive!
The dear lady had kept the phone listing in my father's,
her husband's, name! There was no need for another long
series of inquiries. No more lies, no more excuses, no
more danger of blundering into a brother or uncle and
having to cover up. Everything aboveboard.

All I had to do was deal with the final dilemma: how best to make the contact. I had never allowed myself to think ahead seriously to exactly what I would do when I had found her. The search had gone on so long that, although I certainly hoped with all the force of my being that there would be final identification, the actual formation of a plan for that vital communication would have seemed to be tempting fate. A searching adoptee learns to take one step at a time. There was now more than fleeting fear.

Did I really want to contact her now that all that stood between us was a telephone number? I had never had any overwhelming thoughts that I had been rejected as a baby, nor did I harbour any sense of resentment, but was I prepared for rejection at this stage? But I had not worked for so long to let my fears stop me now. I was a middle-aged adult and felt strongly that if I took this next step with care and sensitivity a successful contact could be made without my intruding unfeelingly into her life. Any response which I had coming to me would be better than not knowing anything.

But what to do? There were several things to consider. Mrs. Attwood — Alleyne — my mother, was not young, she might be ill, or in no condition to cope with the shock of a call from a long-lost daughter. How could I find out? The first step was to confirm that this indeed was the right person before barging in.

I called the town office and asked for the name of the person to whom the house at that address was registered. The secretary had some difficulty in deciding if this was or was not public information. I reminded her of the voters' rolls that in the weeks leading up to the previous

election had been posted on telephone poles all over the
province. Surely nothing could be more public than that.
She still hesitated. Silently I railed at her indecision. *Come
on, lady,* I said to myself, *all I am asking is a name. I have the
address. Just one little name, please.* I asked aloud, "Could
you give me the names of the voters at that address?" She
hemmed and hawed and then — finally! — told me that
the house was registered to an Alleyne Hilda Attwood.

When I heard the name I knew there was no doubt, no
doubt whatsoever, that I had found my birth mother. The
name was the final confirmation. She had given me her
name, as my father had given me his.

I still had to find an answer to my second question: her
state of health. As a child, I had gone to a summer camp
run by a woman from this same small town. We had kept
in touch over the past twenty-five years, sending Christmas cards and the odd letter, but I had not seen her since
I was fifteen. I hesitated, then decided to call her. Small
towns being what they are, the chances were relatively
good that she would know my birth mother, or at least
know of her. I felt that I shared a professional bond of
confidentiality with her. I knew if I asked her about my
birth mother, and she did know her, she would never
betray my trust.

I told her of my search, and of the certain identification
of Alleyne Attwood as my birth mother. She was surprised, for not only did she know my birth mother but,
she told me, her son was one of Alleyne's younger son's
best friends. Son? Younger son? "She has two sons?"
"Yes, and two daughters." I had two brothers and two
sisters! My friend told me that my mother was a fine
person, was an active, healthy, kind, lovely woman, a

retired dietician who still did consulting work and wrote a column for the local paper. "She is quiet, reserved, but lots of fun." What a small world — to think that someone I had known since childhood knew my birth mother. That her son, whom I remembered as a little boy at camp, had grown up with my brother.

I have no idea how long I just sat in my office digesting this information. My mother I had known about, and I knew my father was dead, but the existence of siblings had been a hazy concept. I knew there had been at least one — from that elusive birth announcement — but *four*! I desperately hoped I could meet them, but I would never contact them without my birth mother's permission.

One can't just barge into a person's life. That, however, is exactly what I was contemplating. Should I do it myself, or find someone else to make the first contact? But who? It would be asking too much of my old camp director, even though she was the only person I knew who knew us both, and who knew the story. No, it was my problem, my decision, and I had to follow it through to the end.

As the search wound down, I had felt compelled to tell the friends who had been so supportive — my friends in Waterloo, Guelph, Toronto, London, my cousin in Toronto, and others. They had all heard about my definite identification of my father a short time before, and now they each got another call. I wanted to shout it to the world, "I've found them! I have two brothers and two sisters!" Somehow, I never took seriously the possibility of having to phone them back to say, "She didn't want to meet me."

Over the years I had been in touch with a member of

Parent Finders, a wonderful girl who had given me encouragement when I needed it. She had been my only contact with another adoptee. When I called her that evening and told her that I had located my birth mother, her joy for me reached out and touched my heart over the telephone line from Toronto.

"How do I contact her? Do I telephone or do I write?" A letter seemed so cold and impersonal — and so easy to ignore. If I wrote I might never know her reaction. I decided to telephone, so that at least I would hear her voice.

Marjorie told me what to say. I copied down the formula recommended by Parent Finders as she dictated it to me. She recommended that I wait until the next morning before telephoning. It isn't wise to call last thing at night, because she might be tired and I couldn't be sure how she would react. Also, a call in the morning, when other members of the household are likely to be away at work, is more private. I went to bed that night counting the hours until morning. The next morning I watched the hands of the clock move (incredibly slowly) towards ten (the suggested magic hour). I thought of the hackneyed saying, which is now so popular on posters . . . *Today is the first day of the rest of your life.*

My secretary (who is also a close friend) was in the next day, and at five to ten I went upstairs from our recreation room office with her "Good luck!" ringing in my ears. Taking the phone on its long cord from the hall to my comfortable chair in the living room, I set it on my grandmother's petit-point stool. The sun streamed through the bay window; the cat was asleep on the couch, and the dog was stretched out in a patch of sunlight on the rug. Both blissfully carrying on with their lives in the comfortable way that animals have. I looked hesitatingly at the phone.

I dialled carefully. This was not the time to reach a wrong number . . . The line was busy! How could she be on the phone! I poured two cups of coffee and returned to the office, where I went through the motions of dealing with mail. Fifteen minutes later I mounted the stairs again. The dog and the cat hadn't moved. This time the line was clear. As I listened to it ring I looked down at my notes. First I would introduce myself professionally, then follow the Parent Finders formula.

She answered. "Alleyne Attwood."

"This is Madelene Allen speaking. I am the director of Camp Ouareau, and I am calling from Lennoxville, Quebec. I am calling you on a very personal matter, is it convenient for you to talk?" (I was remembering the advice I had been given, "Give the person a chance to back off. Maybe this is the morning of the Tupperware party! If the response is that this is not a good time, make arrangements to call back, and be sure to leave your phone number, but don't push it then.")

"Yes."

"I am an adult adoptee, and a member of a group known as Parent Finders. Are you familiar with the organization?" ("Give her time to slowly absorb what may be coming. If at this point she recognizes the name Parent Finders she will immediately know who you are and why you are calling, and you will be spared any further speech. Be prepared for her to hang up. Sometimes people hang up out of shock at the point when realization sets in. Don't give up, call back, and sweetly say, 'I'm afraid we were cut off,' and if they hang up again you have a problem.")

"No, I am not familiar with it." *(Oh, help! This wasn't going to be easy.)*

"It is a national group of adoptees, adoptive parents and birth parents who are active in reunions and who have great concern with the present government legislation. . . ."

My throat was dry. I wished I had thought to bring a glass of water to have at hand. My thoughts raced as I read from my text. *How did I ever get into this? I am making a terrible mistake. My voice doesn't sound like my own. She doesn't want to talk to me, I know she will hang up. What will I do if she does? This is ridiculous.* I paused, waiting . . . there was silence at the other end. I continued to read from my notes; my mind had ceased to function on its own.

"I was born on July 3, 1942," I read, "in Barrie, Ontario, and my birth name was Alleyne Patricia Attwood. I have discovered through several years of research that my father's name was Walter Ernest Attwood."

I stopped. I had been advised to say my piece, then "shut up and listen. Don't say another word. Wait, and wait, and wait. You are a voice out of the past — there will be a great deal going on in her mind. Give her time to react." I waited. It seemed forever, but I don't suppose it was more than about thirty seconds.

At last she replied. "It really must be Patricia. How wonderful."

I will never, ever forget that sentence. She wasn't going to reject me! She was not angry at being found. Merely to hear my mother say my name was the most wonderful sound in the world.

"Won't the others be surprised!"

No discussion, no questioning, simply that she was going to tell my brothers and sisters, and that meant I would meet them. This was an indication of the love and the security of a unique family.

Later, my birth mother told me that she didn't remember my saying anything after my date of birth, or "I didn't hear the rest!"

We talked for almost an hour. I don't remember the conversation in any great detail, except that we briefly exchanged information about our lives. I learned about my brothers and sisters, their jobs, their children. I was an aunt six times over! We arranged a meeting for the weekend of May 12, three weeks away, the first weekend my husband was free so that we could drive up together. It happened to be Mother's Day.

After hanging up I just sat, for I know not how long. I was drained, overwhelmed, and ecstatic. I floated down the stairs to the office and Sandy's waiting ears, and recounted the details. I called my husband at work, my friends, I told the dog, the cat — I could not contain my joy. My search was actually over. I had found her! The quest that had been such a huge part of my life had come to an end. The let-down would set in later, but for now I could look ahead to the meeting. Now there was a new stage: the beginning.

9

REUNION

Those who reduce the adoptee's
compelling need for his true identity to a
mere "curiosity," or a search for another
or better mother, are cruelly unaware of
this basic human need to be attached to
one's true place in history.
A.D. Sorosky et al., *The Adoption Triangle:*
The Effect of Sealed Records

M Y LIFE HAD been so centred on the actual search and
the goal of reunion that when it was completed I
simply wrote in my notebook "the rest is history," as if
that was the end of emotion, the end of recorded fact.
There had been so many letters, so much writing, so
much hunting, so many phone calls — it just seemed that
there was nothing else that had to be noted. I wish now
that I had kept a diary for the five years since that time.

Reunion. The time leading up to the actual meeting
was a period filled with apprehension and fear, with the
overwhelming realization of what I had done. Once I had
met my family a great sense of peace came over me and

filled my life. Almost within an hour of finding my birth family, I no longer felt I had to prove myself. The monkey was off my back. The genealogical confusion was gone. The link with my past had been made and the details would soon be known. Negative feelings, with the accompanying guilt, were left behind as it became clear that my birth family was indeed overjoyed at the family being reunited.

The excitement of waiting three weeks to meet them was too much to bear. My husband, the calmest and most cautious of men, surprised me by suggesting that, instead of waiting on tenterhooks, I phone my birth mother back that same night and inquire if I could go to meet her the next Monday (this was Thursday). I was afraid of being pushy, but decided that he was right — postponing it three weeks more, after waiting for so long, was just too much. I was also unrealistically afraid that they might change their minds! I called her back, and she was delighted at the thought, even though it advanced, to the immediate present, her problem of how to tell my siblings that "there had been another." I was to hear the story of that family conference in her kitchen several days later. It was proof of the love and strength of the new family I was entering that their reaction was . . . if it made their mother happy, then they, too, would welcome me.

And what a welcome it was. I flew to Toronto, rented a car, and drove northward. Memories came flooding back as I drove up that familiar road, for the first sixty miles had been the route to our summer cottage, and as I child I had gone up and down this highway with my parents every summer for years. Snippets of long-forgotten conversations with Mom and Dad came back to my mind. I remembered reading *Anne of Green Gables* on this road, our little dachshund cuddling into my side in the back seat, snoring gently until, like magic, he would awaken for the last mile and bark furiously with joy. I remembered the anticipation of showing a new friend my secret places in the woods. Like a ruffled deck of cards these memories fluttered between thoughts of meeting my new family.

Finally, the four-lane highway turned into a winding two-lane road. I have always felt an almost mystical attachment to Canadian Shield country, and here they were, living not in a strange landscape but in the midst of an area that I loved. The anticipation during that hour and a half from the airport was excruciating; it was equal to all those other traumatic periods in one's life: the night before final exams, the night before your wedding, the last week or two before your first child is born. No, it was like all of them rolled into one.

I checked into the hotel on the edge of town, for I had decided it would be too much too soon to expect to stay with them right off. What if I didn't like them? What if they didn't like me? I sat down on the edge of the bed and lifted the receiver. My birth mother's friendly voice on the other end greeted me and asked me, in the way that all mothers have, if I had had a safe trip. Replying in the affirmative (little did she know how little my mind had been on the road), I asked her for directions to her house and said I would be over after lunch. (There are some things that you simply cannot do on an empty stomach.) Taking just long enough to run a comb through my hair, and dig my book out of my suitcase (as a compulsive reader I never eat alone in a restaurant without a book), I headed down to the restaurant.

As I read, club sandwich partway to my mouth, I was suddenly aware of someone watching me. I raised my eyes, and they locked with those of a small, friendly-looking woman who *looked like me!*

Coming towards me, she said, "I couldn't wait." We embraced as if it were the most natural thing in the world to do — which of course it was. The dining room was crowded; it was not a private moment by any means, but Alleyne told me afterwards she was not aware of anyone else in the room and had recognized me immediately. She wrote in a letter to close friends a few days afterwards: "I had the most all-encompassing feeling of what I can only express as 'completeness.'"

She sat down and ordered a coffee while I finished my lunch. We chatted together like two old friends, but I have absolutely no recollection of what we talked about. I signed the chit and I followed her "home."

My sister from Toronto — Gail — was standing on the side porch when I turned into the driveway. She smiled and waved. I got out of the car somewhat hesitatingly. What does one do when a full sister, whom you have never met, is actually standing ten feet from you? I didn't have to worry for she approached me with outstretched arms. There was no doubt it was my sister — *she looked like me!* My eleven-year-old nephew was home from school with a cold — a natural, friendly kid. I have never ceased to be amazed at the ease with which my nieces and nephews accepted me from the beginning — their Long-Lost Aunt. I have two new nieces and nephew now, who will never remember when Aunt Madelene, or Aunt

Ferg (the family is split between my given name and my nickname), wasn't part of the family. But for these other six there was no shyness, no embarrassment; I was me, they were themselves, and we were all part of the same family.

My second sister, Libby, came home from work early. There was no doubt that she was my sister — *I looked like her.* Another warm, tender, friendly, welcoming hug. Then my two brothers came in half an hour apart. The older of the two, Jim, was training to be a nurse at the hospital where I was born. He gave me a little parcel containing what is now one of my most prized possessions, a little pink baby shirt with the words *I Was Born at Royal Victoria Hospital* emblazoned across the front. And Jeff — I will never forget the look on his face as he came into the kitchen and looked at us all sitting around the kitchen table. "Well, she certainly is an Attwood!" I wish I had had a tape recorder going that afternoon, for all I remember is the laughter and an overwhelming feeling of comfort in being together.

There was a great deal of laughter surrounding the story of how my mother had told them about me. My deciding to come three weeks earlier than first planned had put her in the position of having to tell the family straightaway about the existence of another sister. She had planned to go down to Toronto on the Friday to spend the day with my sister, Gail, as her husband had just left on a business trip to England, and to return with her and her two young sons the next day. So the meeting had to be the night I had called. The poor woman had had hardly any time to pull her thoughts together! My brother was playing basketball until 10:30 p.m., so it was arranged that he would go home, pick up his wife, and come round to her house as soon as possible. Nursing exams were looming on the horizon for my older brother. He would take one hour off from studying to watch his favourite television show, which finished at 11:00. She decided to talk to the two boys first, and then tell the girls together on their return from Toronto the next evening. Refusing to tell the boys anything over the telephone, she arranged the meeting. All she would say was that she had something very important to discuss with them. They were terrified that perhaps she had a serious medical problem, so when it turned out that there was nothing wrong they were relieved — the implications of a new sister were minor in comparison.

In her account, she wrote: "Their reaction was that if I was happy about it, they thought it was just fantastic — complete and absolute acceptance. We talked a little about the ramifications, then left further thought about it until I told the girls." She went on to describe the disclosure to my sisters: "I didn't say anything to Gail, even on the drive back although I was tempted, but waited until Saturday night after her children were in bed. The boys came over just as I concluded and were there to hear them say exactly what they had. Wonderful! Great! When will we meet her? I was proud of them and love them all so much." How could she have had the self-control to wait for two whole days to tell my sisters?

I was so gratified to read in her letter that "she belongs — and it wasn't very long before *all* of us had this incredible sensation of having known her forever."

I went back to the hotel that night after supper, leaving them a biography and a six-page outline of what I had done to find them. In one way I wanted to stay with them for the evening, but we all needed an emotional break from each other. I watched television for a while, but couldn't keep my mind on the trivia on the screen. The events on "The National" held no interest for me — what was the significance of world news on a night when my world had changed. I snapped off the TV, had a long soak in a welcoming tub and crawled into bed. I dug out my notebook, which I had brought to show them, and wrote the final entry:

It is unbelievable. I feel as if I have come home. I'm numb, I'm happy, I'm exhausted — mentally and physically — but at last, I am part of my family. That hardly sounds fair to my adoptive parents — I was a part and I am a part of them, but more as if I was "on loan" rather than "as if born." I feel so grateful — I have never felt such warmth — such an outpouring of "you belong." To look at them and see myself mirrored in each — a little different — but to hear each say, "You're an Attwood." How can strangers become sudden family? We know nothing of each other and yet here we are. It seems too good to be true.

The next morning I checked out of the hotel and went back to the neat little white house on the quiet dead-end street. It was a joyous day. I played tourist with my mother, driving around town, visiting the local wildlife centre, meeting special neighbours, going through old photograph albums, chatting about this and that. Both of us trying, almost frantically, to get caught up on the events of the last forty years. I had brought pictures of my family, and of myself as a child. The thing that impressed me most that day was how at ease we felt together. There was a great deal of conversation, but there were also comfortable silences that no one felt the need to fill.

The next evening we sat with the outline of my search spread on the kitchen table. My mother held up the non-identifying information and said, "No wonder you had such problems. They have my age wrong!" I had been absolutely right when I thought that certain facts did not hang together. Her date of birth, as I had calculated it, was out by two years. Thus, my technique of eliminating female Attwoods by the years of their birth, although logically correct, would never have come up with the right answer because I was looking in the wrong years. I doubt if I would have started again on the premise that the age was wrong for I had asked again and again for verification of data and the error had been made during the compilation of the data back in 1942. I was so lucky to have found her!

My mother gave me a very special gift, a letter that my father had written *to me* before I was born, while he was on leave in England. It was a short note written on a package of pictures from the King Arthur legend. He spoke of love, of our future life together, of joy. He had never thought that they would have to give me up. When I showed this very private letter to my sister some months later she told me that he had been a wonderful correspondent. No other letters have been seen from that time (not that any of us have asked) but my birth mother had kept that letter. She told me that they had never spoken of me once I had gone, but she was never able to throw away that note. "Maybe, subconsciously, I thought I might give it to you some day." Although I "missed" my father by twenty years, he has touched my life and my heart. This visit filled in the gaps and tied the loose ends of my life together. Shortly before my father had gone overseas in 1941, my mother had found that she was pregnant and as she wrote in her letter to friends announcing my "second arrival":

... so you can well imagine it was a very upsetting and trying time for him across the sea. He managed — somehow — to get a transfer back in May of 1942 and on July 3rd we had a daughter. Wallie was married, altho' he and his wife had separated before the war began. He had left Canada for South Africa where he was to set up a branch for Sun Life. He visited his parents for six weeks in England and it was so obvious from that perspective that war was imminent, that he changed his plans and returned to Canada to rejoin the reserve. They were trying times. Although we wanted to marry, he was not divorced; he did not know where he would be posted and I was awaiting acceptance into the army. We had the baby with us for two weeks, then through Dr. Hassard, mother and dad's doctor, we placed her in the Mothercraft hospital trying to figure out what was best for her. Dr. Hassard had friends who wanted to adopt a child, and under his guidance this was arranged through the Children's Aid. She was a beautiful child and we knew that hard as it was for both of us, that she was going to the kind of home that we would have wanted to give her, and we knew that we were doing the right thing.

There was the final accounting. A truly heartbreaking story, and I admire my mother for being able to write this so clearly and thoughtfully forty-three years later and for sharing this letter with me. She had told me these facts, but to see them written down gave them a greater clarity. I had had so many new experiences, stories, facts flung at me over the forty-eight hours of my visit that I appreciated seeing some of them in print.

I asked her if she had ever thought of trying to get in touch with me, and she replied simply, "No, it was not my place to do that." She did comment that with the amount of publicity about adoption in the mid-1980s she sometimes wondered if we ever might meet. She told me that she had driven by the house once, just to see where I was living. I had known that my birth father had tried on one occasion to meet with my adoptive father, when I was seven or eight, just to find out how I was. His overture was firmly rebuffed, and they never met.

I returned home to Lennoxville, my soul at peace. Two weeks later my husband and I returned to Ontario for a very special Mother's Day. This only child sat down to lunch with fifteen family members.

My mother wrote to Parent Finders in August after another reunion during camp. She had seen the place that has meant so much to me over the past thirty years, and at last had met my children. I am sure that she will not object to my sharing the feelings of a birth mother with the world:

Thank you Parent Finders, so very much, for the big part you played in bringing our two families together. It has been an unbelievable, happy time for us all. Why must it be such a difficult procedure? I realize that not all such reunions are happy ones, nor long-lasting, as I know ours is going to be, but there must be ways of anticipating the problem ones and at least making them private events. Ours — we wanted the whole world to know. What a wonderful girl she is.

I don't know whether Madelene has written at length to you, but she may have told you of all the strange interaction of people and events and places that we have discovered. We all have so much in common.

(This appeared in *P.F.I. Communiqué*, Vol. 9, #2, Oct. 1985)

10

THE END WAS ONLY
A BEGINNING

In general, it is the policy of the law to
make the veil between past and present
lives of adopted persons as opaque and
impenetrable as possible, like the veil
which God has placed between the living
and the dead.

English court, 1956

OUR LIVES ARE divided into compartments, each marked by a beginning and an end. For every beginning there must be an ending of the phase that precedes it. Not until this process has been completed can one begin the next stage. Society has created a number of traditions for these rites of passage. A graduation ceremony marking the end of high school helps us say goodbye to friends and to a way of life and the innocence of youth. A religious or civil ceremony formalizes a marriage and blesses the new family; relatives and friends are present to display support and approval. If we change jobs, move, or retire, there must also be time to say goodbye — we can't just walk away. Without this process there is an emptiness and an unsettledness which remains until the passage of time heals the wounds or simply covers them.

Any major life change causes a deep sense of upheaval and of displacement, psychological or otherwise. What greater life change could there be than finding and melding into a new family? This is totally different from the blended families created as a result of divorce and remarriage, for we are dealing with blood relatives and all the emotional baggage — on both sides — of the years since the birth of the adopted child. Birth, marriage, job changes, death, all these happenings within normal life are contained within our frame of reference. They happen in our families and in those of our friends, and they demarcate clear and well-defined stages in our lives. But a "first" family? A reunion with a family we were never supposed to meet? We have no experience on which to base our reactions — nor do our friends. There is no established rite-of-passage ceremony to mark such an event.

The act of telling friends and family was certainly a self-created rite, but unlike other, more usual ceremonies, this one was sometimes greeted with doubt. "I hope you have done the right thing." "I hope you won't be hurt." "I hope you won't be disappointed." Right to the end there were a few warnings of possible disillusionment. No one ever makes those comments to a newly married couple! Just as marriage launches you into a new life, so does reunion with a new family. My discovery of them and theirs of me, our mutual establishment of a familial relationship, had to happen gradually. Friends and family had to wait to be reassured.

It was strange, but at this period I found myself remembering more and more things about my growing years, and about Mom and Dad, that I had not thought of for years. I remembered tiny things — a smile, a vignette of a dinner table, a quiet walk. These memories did not come to haunt, but to comfort me in a time of upheaval, a necessary period of adaptation.

The discovery of my new family marked the beginning of a new stage in my life — one that was no less significant than any other I had experienced. No less momentously, it marked the end of my search: a search that had consumed every free moment that I could squeeze from the past one thousand, four hundred and sixty days; a search that had been the driving force of my life for the past four years, and that had started seven years before that. This could not simply be put aside like a ski jacket when the warmth of spring arrives. Even with the joy of the reunion, and all the excitement of getting to know my new family, I could not deny an overwhelming let-down.

It was time to pick up the other threads in my life, to get involved in other things. The search, despite its frustrations, had been fun and I enjoyed it. It had been the ultimate mystery game, with no flipping to the last page to see "who done it." Well, I *had* done it, and now it was finished, and there was no encore, no replay. The notebooks were forever closed. I had to find a time-consuming project in my life until nature took its course and allowed me to gear down. I deliberately started a major project to revise our camp staff manual. Even when that was done, three months later, I still felt an empty space.

It is not always easy to judge the reactions of family and friends, and I was not as aware as I should have been of the effects that my finding my family had on those who were close to me. Just recently one of my closest friends confided that at the time she was afraid that our friendship might suffer, and that it took her some time to get used to my referring to "my brother" or "my sister" in conversation. She is an only child, and we had considered each other "the sister we never had." She had been close to me throughout the search; I valued her support during those difficult years. She rejoiced with me, but it was an adjustment for her, too. The last thing in the world I would ever want is to hurt this special friend; but now I realize that I was insensitive to her feelings. It was something that should have been addressed directly.

I know that I have been remiss in keeping contact with some of my more distant relatives. It is a question of time. Now, the extra two days on a trip to Toronto are taken up with a trip to see my family, not darting around the countryside to see other, scattered relatives.

My only lingering sadness is that I "missed" my father. I know that he was a strong, loving family man, for they speak of how his example of family loyalty and support helped them through the difficult times after his death in 1964. He led an adventuresome life before settling down in his second marriage. I have before me his *Officer's Declaration Papers* from December, 1941. He has listed his previous war service during the First World War in tiny, formal script: "(1916-17) Military Transport, Salonika, Egypt, Australia, South Africa, (1917-18): Served eight months in France. (1918-19) H.M. Coldstream Guards. Discharged, Feb. 1919. Rejoined Military Transport proceeding to evacuation of Archangel, Murmansk, Russia." What stories he must have been able to tell . . . or was he like my adoptive father, who never spoke of his three years in the trenches?

My son is now the proud owner of two First World War service medals. One from the Canadian army that was my father's, the other my birth father's from the Merchant Marine, commemorating the Russian evacuations, which my birth mother gave him as a "welcome to the family" gift.

After the Mother's Day visit, we exchanged letters. At first they were biographical, with questions and answers going back and forth, but before long they became typical family letters — who was doing what, comments on the events and politics of the day, discussions of family plans. I had letters of welcome from various friends and relations in response to the letter that Alleyne had written to all of them broadcasting her joy at being found. I never ceased to be amazed by her openness, which makes a mockery of the argument that records must be sealed to protect the anonymity of the birth parents. Why doesn't the government ask birth parents their real feelings? Perhaps as the Adoption Disclosure Registry does its work, there will be a realization that all this happened so long ago that emotions have calmed, society has changed, and the related problems are not as serious as was once expected. As my mother said, she did not feel that my appearance on the stage of her life at this point would make any difference whatsoever to how people viewed her. It had all happened forty years ago; she had made her reputation and people are understanding of what can and did happen during wartime. This is the greatest myth concerning sealed records. I realize that mine is just one case, but there are hundreds if not thousands of birth parents who are members of Parent Finders groups across North America, and the system should reflect their choice of openness.

My appearance affected my brothers and sisters, too, and they seemed to go out of their way to say "you belong." My younger sister had made my mother a sampler when her first grandchild was born, with his name and birth date, and had continued to add embroidered names with each new addition to the family. Almost immediately after our reunion Gail managed to find space at the top to insert the names of the two new oldest grandchildren. She also sent me a copy of a revised family tree shortly after the reunion, with me, my husband, and our children included. It was these tiny tangible indications that meant so much and that formalized our new unit. These were the substance of the rites of passage — for all of us. The things that marked the beginning of our new life together. It was not until I saw the family tree that I realized that the previous "eldest" was known by her middle name, and that we share the same first name — Alleyne.

As we spend more time together we realize that we have much more than names in common. The old argument of heredity versus environment should be examined in a situation involving adoption reunion. We have had a lot of fun identifying similarities. I will never forget the first evening we had together. I have often been teased about my habit of emphasizing a point by gesturing with my right hand. During an Attwood conversation there is a great deal of right-hand-waving! One would have thought that sort of habit was picked up subconsciously, by imitating one's parents — but it seems that it can be transmitted in the genes.

Despite our different backgrounds, we find that we have similar senses of humour, tend to have the same life philosophy, and relate to others alike. We have common interests and hobbies — all the family are outdoor types. When my mother first visited the camp she immediately went for an energetic swim in our cold Laurentian lake, then set off in a canoe before dinner. Canoeing had been a passion of mine and I worked at the camp for a number of years as head of the canoeing program and as a tripper. My daughter is now our tripper. No wonder we have blended so well as a re-created family. Professionally, we are in similar fields. I have been a teacher and camp director all my working life, as well as having a fundamental love for the out-of-doors. Lib, the elder of my two "little" sisters, is deeply involved in the running of a wildlife centre, my brother Jeff is a teacher and involved in physical education, the other brother, Jim, is a psychiatric nurse dealing with outpatient and community care in a clinic, and my younger sister Gail is the artistic one of the family — a talented painter, carver, and craftsperson.

We were amazed, as we compared notes, at the coincidences of mutual friends. I have mentioned my old camp director, but my daughter's godmother grew up in my birth parents' small town, and they knew her father. The heartbreaking irony of another coincidence was that my sister and her husband had been transferred to Quebec in the 1970s. She had been desperately homesick and would have given anything for family nearby; at the time, I was recovering from back surgery and to me, too, family would have meant so much — and there we were, exactly an hour's drive away from each other. The cruelty of the conspiracy of silence!

That first summer my mother and two sisters came up to camp for a wonderful visit. This was the first time that they had seen me on "my turf." There was a communion of spirit that had never been so evident before. We had moved into a phase of calm acceptance of the inevitability, the permanence, and the rightness of what had happened. One glorious windy day I took Gail for her first sail. We sped down the lake, laughing like two teenagers.

Neither my mother nor I had told them of the letter from my father. I had shown it to my husband, but no one else. It was too precious to be shared widely. I showed it to my sisters individually during those few days of peace in the Laurentian mountains. There were tears in our eyes as they remembered the man they knew as Dad, and they wept for his heartbreak and the loss of his dream of this first girl child. I had never wished more fervently in my life that I could roll back time and meet him. I hope that there is some way that he knows what has happened. If there is any justice, and any eternal love, he *must*.

My brother Jim and I came to the conclusion that, if I had grown up in the family, we would have been the bane of our father's existence, for we were both rabble-rousers who tended to defy traditional authority. Jim also came to camp that summer. A senior staff member identified him the minute he walked into camp, and another friend pointed out that seeing us from the back you could tell we were related for we carry ourselves the same way. We had spent very little time alone together until that visit, but in those two days we became brother and sister. It was uncanny. We found that we could almost complete each other's sentences, as if we had grown up together, as if the intervening years had never existed. I feel a real closeness to all of my siblings, but I am sure they will agree that they too see this special empathy.

I felt for some time that I had to tread softly. It all seemed too good to be true. Did they really want me, or was I intruding? Were they just being nice? How long did they want me to stay? Would it all wear off? These doubts and questions are inevitable, I think, but after repeated visits and letters my fears and trepidation melted away. My sisters shared their thoughts about their growing up and about my joining the family in several letters, which helped me to believe in my acceptance in the family. It may seem strange, but despite the outward assurances, the natural comfortableness, I still wondered deep down if this wonderful reunion was truly possible. Reason, however, came to my aid and told me that they would not just "be polite" about something so significant. Gail wrote, several months after our meeting:

There was no reason for us to feel any type of animosity towards you. You didn't come looking for us to step on any toes. You came as a stranger looking for birth connections and a chance to squelch your curiosity — "seek and ye shall find." You had a lot of courage — you didn't know what you would find or how you would be accepted. You were the underdog. But you had no say in your creation or the subsequent circumstances. I knew how strong the feelings were in our family — although very rarely mentioned — Dad and Mom instilled a sense of love and caring into four fairly young children before Dad died and Mom carried on teaching us with a quiet understanding. So I guess when I heard about you, there was mainly a feeling of loss for Mom and Dad (imagine the pain

of separating), and then wow, who is She, what is
She, When, Where and we all knew the Why. And
now Mom was going to be able to see you. If Mom
had let us, I'm sure we all would have been waiting
on the front porch that first day! But we didn't want
to overwhelm you. That day is clear in my mind,
meeting you, sitting outside, and then one by one
the others coming to meet you, the glances and the
hugs, the acceptance, the oneness of a family. I'm
only sorry that Dad isn't alive to see you. He would
have been proud of the way you were raised. I'll
always remember his pride in us and the way he
instilled pride in ourselves and whatever job we do.
Well done, Madelene! You worked hard and long,
you kept it up, and look what you have found.

How could I harbour any doubt after that outpouring of
warmth and understanding?
Lib sent me a photostat of a letter she wrote to a friend.

An older sister, what a strange feeling! For all the
years of responsibility for younger brothers and
sister, here was an older sister suddenly on the
scene — to take this responsibility away? — to share
it? — to be a friend? My emotions were very near
the surface (an unusual experience for me who is
always in control). My heart went out to my mother
and father. Putting myself in their places I could feel
my father's anguish at having to give up their child.
There was nothing so precious as Dad's children.
Through all his illness and anger at himself and the
world he always cared for us. He taught us *absolute*

respect for Mom and all other elders, and yet encouraged us too, to learn as much as we could within his guidelines. Mom's happiness though, when Madelene contacted her, was enough to overcome all doubts. I am sure a part of her is now complete and that to me is of prime importance. And to find, too, another two grandchildren (especially with Bruce looking so much like Mom's side of the family) is marvellous! I hope, as the years go by, that we can all learn to know each other better and build into the future.

That was five years ago. I have had time to contemplate the significance of family, and I am sure that I will never come up with a definitive summation or explanation of what has occurred. My children, as brother and sister, will have a relationship with each that is completely different from mine with *my* brothers and sisters and always will be, simply because of the fact that they have grown up together. They have fought, played, dealt with jealousy and anger, and now as young adults have become friends. None of this childhood and adolescent baggage is part of my relationship with my siblings. But how is it that we can with so *little* difficulty identify each other as brothers and sisters, when we lost those childhood and young adult years completely? Family implies growing up together. But somehow, it is happening. Jim confided in me that he now felt the family was complete, that he had always felt there was something — someone — missing. I believe him, that these were not just kind words to make me feel one of the gang, or a comment made with the advantage of hindsight. I have been assimilated into their family, as they have been assimilated into mine. Does there have to be an explanation for a miracle?

Our lives are now progressing as I would hope all families' lives do — touching, parting, returning. Letters and telephone calls are exchanged regularly. There are visits, not as something extraordinary, but in the normal course of events when family members are forced to live at a distance from one another. My niece has been a camper with us now for the past three years, so visitors' day is a particularly special day for me as well. I have taken friends "home," to visit and to meet my family. These visits are natural, relaxed, and filled with laughter. There are family get-togethers and this past winter our two families and friends met at our twenty-fifth wedding anniversary party. It seemed strange to say to old friends "I'd like you to meet my special mother," but it was a party filled with joy and true reunion. I was saddened by the fact that my parents were not there to join in the festivities, and we remembered them with love. Only one dear friend of my parents felt that she could not cope with the memories under the circumstances. I had to respect her feelings — but it hurt to know that there had been a casualty as a result of my search. There was a price to be paid.

The only slight awkwardness is in use of names. I cannot call my birth mother "Mother," or "Mom." She is Alleyne to my husband and me, and Gram now to my children. I refer to her as "mother" when I am speaking of her to my brothers and sisters, but as a proper noun "Mom" is that wonderful lady who gave me her love for thirty years; the one who comforted me through the trials and tribulations of growing up, who played me to sleep with Chopin, who supported me and chastised me and who was — my mother. Can one have two mothers? I do, and I don't. There is a very special connotation to this word, and no one can ever take "Mom's" place. Alleyne, bless her heart, accepts and understands this. Perhaps one day I will be able to call her Mom, but that will be because of what is happening now. Just as one can have two friends with the same given name, and differentiate between them, so I will differentiate in my heart between my two "Moms."

Our son has just gone off to college not far from his new grandmother's family. He is one of the boys — the cousins are repairing snowmobiles together, going into town, doing the things that cousins do. He is mooching Sunday dinners from the family, as all college students do. He is just another lad who spends time with family when away from home. Our daughter has had a more difficult time accepting the new family for, being older, she remembers my parents in a different way. She has not had the same opportunities for contact with the new family, but as time passes a warmth is growing. My mother has been sensitive in not pushing the relationship or demanding that our daughter immediately bond with her.

I have become a part of the family memories. The greatest honour and the greatest affirmation of my belonging to the family came in 1990 when Jim asked me to propose the toast to "the parents" at his wedding. This was a most unusual experience: standing up as his sister and knowing that most of the people present were aware of my history. However, I did not feel uncomfortable for a moment — I was too proud to be part of that joyous occasion as a sister of the groom.

I began this book by touching on the significance of family heritage and wondering about the stock from which I sprang. I have learned that my grandfather worked for the CPR in Chapleau (the "large Canadian company" — and would I ever have identified him? Never, because his name was Rose, not Attwood). Perhaps the most significant historical gift I have been given is the legacy of Grampa Holding, my maternal great-grandfather. His picture, a copy of a yellowed original, is also hanging on my office wall. He is in profile — a gnarled, bearded old gentleman, pipe clenched between his teeth. He is sitting in the back of a motor boat in a long-sleeved, collarless white shirt with a suit vest over top. The brim of a battered cap is almost parallel with the line of his pipe. Apparently stories still abound in the Chapleau area about this well-known pioneer.

When the family learned of my tenacity and my determination to find them, they paid me what I consider the greatest compliment — they said I must have Holding blood in my veins! Grampa Holding was a survivor. He was born in 1840, and at fourteen ran away from the harsh life of a gamekeeper's son to the even harsher life of the sea. He ended up in Australia, where he spent six years working in the gold fields — a true man from Snowy River. In April, 1864, he signed on to the ill-fated *Invercauld* of Aberdeen to work his passage back to England. The *Invercauld* was wrecked a few days later on the rugged northwest coast of the Auckland Islands, south of New Zealand. He and eighteen others, out of a crew of twenty-three, survived the wreck. A year later, in May of 1865, he, the mate and the skipper were the only ones left to be rescued by a Portuguese ship. He wrote his story, and I am now in the process of gathering information for a book to bring his story to the world — for his memoirs are the only accurate account of this story of heroism and determination. Because of my new family, I am committed to walking those sub-Antarctic islands some time within the next two or three years, in my search for Grampa Holding.

I am part of that family but no less a part of my adoptive family. Part of my spirit still walks the Highland vales of Balquidder and I have been back recently to that silent valley. I stood again by the ancient church and remembered my great-grandparents, who left for the New World, and thought of my great-great-grandparents, who by the emigration of their son had lost him as surely as my birth parents had lost me.

With the same depth of feeling another part of my soul is drawn to the Auckland Islands, where my other great-grandfather suffered and endured. I will walk those islands, and will tell his story. I am twice blessed, for I have two loving families and two heritages, which have made me the person I now know I am.

Appendix I

AN OPEN LETTER

Dear friends from all sides of the triangle,

One of the difficulties with writing this book was that so often I wanted to step out of the role of author and speak directly to you on a personal level, separate from the story and the technical suggestions contained herein. We do not know each other, but likely share a bond — that of searching for unknown relatives, or of working with people deeply involved in a personal quest.

First of all, let me assume that you are another searching adoptee. I understand your frustrations, your anger, your determination.

Have you asked yourself *why* are you searching? If you are searching for a replacement family, or a "better" family, or to punish your adoptive parents, please, stop *now* and save yourself and others profound heartache and distress. No one will replace them, and no one should. It's not fair to expect this of your birth family should you meet them. If you are looking for replacements, you are setting the scene for disaster.

Have you asked yourself *what* you are searching for? Information, you say? What information? Medical? Social? Fair enough, we need this information, but is there another way to get it? No, probably not. I understand, you are tired of waiting.

There is no way to guarantee that your birth parents will register with the Adoption Disclosure Registry, if such exists in your area. When was the last time you saw an ad announcing such a registry? You hope that if they know of it, they will register, but chances are they have never heard of it, and so you have no option but to search.

Have you tried all the other ways? Have you obtained your non-identifying information? Are you sure you want to know more? If counselling services are available, have you made use of them? This doesn't imply that you are "deficient" or unable to cope with the stresses of the situation or your search, but there *are* great benefits in speaking with someone who is abreast of the situation and partially understands our needs. I say partially, for no matter how well educated or how experienced, unless the counsellor is herself adopted, she cannot know the frustration of the genealogical "black hole." However, we can avail ourselves of her empathy and experience.

Do you merely want the satisfaction of a relationship with someone who resembles you? Well, why not? This is a valid desire. You have spent a lifetime with friends and families who constantly display "family resemblances," and every time it's mentioned, a worm of jealousy digs a little deeper into your heart. But don't let that be the *only* reason for your search — there are a lot of strings attached. Is seeing yourself mirrored in other human beings worth the risk? Maybe you won't like them. Maybe they will tell you to take a hike.

Were you adopted as a young child? Do you have a dimly remembered brother or sister from another life? Do you remember a crowded tenement, or simply playing hopscotch with a faceless somebody who was your older sister? What are your emotions: anger, sadness, frustration? How will these emotions translate into interpersonal relations should you actually meet your birth family? Do you have a sense of rejection because you are an adoptee? Are you going to take it out in accusations? No, of course you won't. A long time has passed, but it is worth considering. You are going to have to cope with these emotions.

Have you lain awake and asked yourself what will happen if and when you find them? Have you honestly asked yourself whether you could accept rejection, if it came? There were good reasons why you were placed for adoption. I know, it was a long time ago and times have changed. That is what I have been saying all along, but the possibility remains. Don't get into this if you aren't prepared for any eventuality. Of course, you may be as lucky as I was, but you don't know right now. If you aren't prepared to think ahead, then you are being unrealistic.

What will happen if they do think you are the most wonderful thing since ketchup? Can you accept becoming part of a family? What about responsibilities that may come with that acceptance? Can you cope with whatever situation you may find? Are you willing to keep up with the little commitments that come with being in a family — birthday cards, letters, visits? Will you hold up your end of a relationship when your old life settles back to normal? What about illness or death in this new family? I know I am sounding like your maiden aunt, and the doomsayers that you have talked to. But they do have a point — it can happen. You can cope with all that? Fine. More power to you. Let's be realistic, every family has its griefs and its problems, and if you join a family, it cannot be a superficial relationship. Family implies commitment. It is worth remembering that you are laying this on them, too, if they choose to bring you into the family. They may be a strength to you. Is it fair to them? True, they can always say no . . . So here we are, back at square one.

What kind of a meeting do you want? Can you cope with the fact that their wishes and expectations may not be the same as yours? How will the existence of a "new" family affect your present relationships? How will your present family, spouse, children, cope with the new you, and your new family? You can never know until it happens, but have you discused it with them? Have you dug down through the dreams and the hopes, and delved into the points of reality with your husband, or wife, or significant other? He or she will be involved, too. So will your children. You say that they love you, and are supporting your search — then you probably will have supportive loved ones when you come to the end.

From time to time the awkward question of whether you should be searching at all will creep into your mind. It is hard to deal with the doubters, with the negative societal pressure which is still out there, though thankfully in ever-decreasing doses. You have probably met other adoptees who think you are out of your mind, and you may begin to wonder whether they aren't right. Hang in, and remember each of us is an individual; we react to the curves that life throws us in different ways. There is nothing wrong with wanting to know our past; that has been concluded over and over by wiser minds than ours. If something in your history tells you you must search, then go ahead. As Polonious observed in *Hamlet*, "To thine own self be true, and it must follow as the night the day thou canst not then be false to any man." If we go into our search honestly, openly and trustingly, then we will likely meet those from our past with honesty, openness and trust.

Don't let your non-searching friends put you off. Searching is not for everyone. But for those of us who are driven by the need, it cannot be denied. The suggestion that "good" adoptees do not search and "bad" adoptees do is an anathema. Upon what criteria of evil behaviour are we being judged? If the judge is questioning our loyalty to our birth family, he does not understand the depth of family love nor the depth of our need to know our true heritage.

We must never forget that many lives are bound up in ours and that no family or love damaged is worth our self-knowledge, despite our desire for "rights" and "fairness." We must tread softly, tread with compassion and understanding through the lives of those who nurtured us. We must approach cautiously the lives of those who gave us life. These first parents have made new lives for themselves, either individually or together and we have no special right to upset the balance. You will run into some hotheads who will argue this point, and yes, I have my moments, too, but the bottom line is that we must seriously consider the implications for these other unknowns. We must not be purely selfish. Family security is precious and must not be tampered with.

Accept the fact that it is very hard for our non-adopted friends to understand our discomfort. My husband at first thought it strange that I would search for another family when I had a perfectly good one already. Realize that those who feel uneasy about the whole process of adoption tend to transfer this uneasiness to us, as individuals; we are different in their eyes. They can't enter into our souls, any more than we can enter into theirs. Accept this, and carry on with understanding, grateful for any empathy you can get. You probably have found by now that more people are supportive than are not. Thankfully, the feelings of prejudice against illegitimacy (and let us be honest, most people assume that we were adopted because we were illegitimate, and many of us were!) are becoming less with the changing of mores, but it is still there for many people. It is only by our calmness, determination, and fidelity to the concept of the importance of family — all families — that the public will learn about the necessity of all people knowing their roots.

There are so few guidelines on how to go about a search. You have probably read books galore — if you haven't, start now. Every bit of knowledge will help. Read — gather hints and ideas from every source you can. There are a few handbooks, but each search is so different, so personal, that you will find it necessary to learn as you go along. Do not expect to find the definitive tome that will answer all your questions. If I have been able to help you, even a bit, I am elated.

If you are an adoptive parent, please do not be angry with me. Please do not feel that I have undermined your family. Proportionately, there are just as many sensitive, caring adoptees as there are among the population of non-adoptees. We are not out to get anyone — we are just people with a need. Our discontent and unhappiness is not with you, but in the not knowing. I know you were promised, all those years ago, that the records would never be opened. It seemed very simple when you brought that tiny bundle into your home and into your lives. But does it really matter, now that your child is an adult, an adult who has always been loyal and loving? Do you really think that if she meets her birth mother it will change her feelings towards you? You must have faith that the love you gave to your child was not for naught. Truth and honesty can only strengthen your relationship. Secrecy and evasion about a topic so basic to the family fabric can only give the individual whom you brought into your family with love a sense that there may be something shameful about adoption.

Why must the past rule the present? Your neighbour's children who are "natural" (do you hate the word as much as I?) have grown up with knowledge of their beginnings and of their roots. Shouldn't your own child have that same gift? Why should I as an adoptee be denied the recognition that I am a responsible adult able to cope with whatever knowledge is buried in my past? Surely you who love us, who have always treated us as your own, can accept that we need to know our background and can deal with it — whatever it is. Surely you can accept that the knowledge will not change our relationship with you. Statistics bear this out. We have shared so much, and surely you have enough confidence in your parenting to realize that the love between us is not that shallow. There is a saying that if you love something enough to let it go free, it will return to you. By holding your adopted child, by denying him or her the knowledge of his origin, you are risking the loss of the very thing you are trying to keep. Tell us, be open with us. We will not let you down.

Why was it assumed that we and our birth parents would

never need to know each other, that we would never ask *why* we were surrendered, that our birth parents would never want to know what happened to their child?

Are you a birth parent? Are you afraid of the repercussions? Yes, I am biased, of course — and no, I don't completely understand. But I have seen the joy of my birth mother. Granted, she and my father married, and perhaps you have buried a "mistake," and you too have been assured that the records will never be opened. But try to understand that the child to whom you gave life is now an adult, and has a need to know about her family heritage and all that that entails. Times and attitudes have changed. We won't ask to re-enter your life if that is not what you want, we simply ask to share your knowledge of what directly affects us. Perhaps it's not fair that it has all been raked up again. You tried to forget about it, but we have to live with it — we *are* "it." Please try to understand our need, the need to know about *you*. Keep it anonymous, by all means. We won't barge in. But please take the time at least to share your knowledge.

If you are a searching birth parent, keep at it. You are not alone by any means. In a survey conducted in the United States of 170 reunions, 70 percent were initiated by birth parents searching for their children. This survey asked: "If you could go back in time but knew you couldn't change anything, would you still reunite?" The proportion of searching and non-searching birth parents who said yes was 98 percent (Silverman et al., *Reunions between Adoptees and Birth Parents*).

A final encouraging note, from the abovementioned book: "Contrary to expectation, reunions do not seem to disrupt the lives of the participants. Even birth mothers who did not search and who still would not do so were pleased to be found. At least from the point of view of the birth parents the reunion, even if unsuccessful, seems to enhance their lives."

So, my friends from all sides of the adoption triangle, more power to you. None of us asked for the trials and tribulations of being, or being involved with, a searching adoptee or birth parent. We are not easy people to deal with because we believe so deeply in what we are doing. Please trust us.

Appendix II

SEARCH
INFORMATION

I. SEARCH AND SUPPORT GROUPS

   A. PARENT FINDERS

From the Parent Finders of Canada newsletter:

Parent Finders began in Vancouver in 1974, to provide a support group to adult adoptees, birth relatives and adopting parents. [They are active in most provinces and have strong contacts with activist groups throughout the United States, England and Australia — Author.]

The primary aim of Parent Finders is to promote a feeling of openness and understanding about the whole concept of adoption. The services include:

- general counselling
- direction on where to obtain background information
- information assistance in search
- providing, where requested, skilled intermediaries to make a discreet first contact to the party being sought
- maintaining the Canadian Adoption Reunion Register (CARR) wherein birth information can be confidentially filed.

To July 1989, there are over 24,000 registrations in CARR and over 4,000 reunions have been recorded. A reunion survey done in 1979 showed that 92 percent of all birth mothers contacted were grateful for the opportunity for a reunion, 88 percent of birth fathers were pleased to be contacted and 99 percent of birth sisters and 97 percent of birth brothers were pleased to participate in the reunion experience. These percentages continue to apply.

The Parent Finders address: Parent Finders of Canada, National Headquarters, 3960 Westridge Avenue, West Vancouver, B.C. V7V 3H7. For the chapter in your area consult your telephone book, or contact the national office.

B. TRIAD (Society for Truth in Adoption of Canada)
From the TRIAD newsletter:

TRIAD is a non-profit charitable volunteer organization dedicated to reuniting families who have become separated, usually through the adoption process. Operating costs are covered by nominal membership fees, donations and fundraising events. It offers the following services:

- information regarding post-adoption services offered by provincial governments
- affiliation with CARR and ISRR (International Soundex Reunion Registry)
- newsletter which provides search techniques, legislative updates, general information and news regarding adoption, articles and search ads
- monthly meetings
- direction and support in your search.

The Triad national address: TRIAD, National Office, Box 5922, Station B, Victoria, B.C. V8R 6S8. There are chapters of TRIAD in Chatham, Ontario; Calgary, Alberta; and Victoria, B.C.

C. JIGSAW INTERNATIONAL

JIGSAW International is affiliated with Parent Finders and similar organizations in the United States. Their address: Jigsaw International, 39 Manifold Road, Blackett, Sydney, Australia.

II. INDEPENDENT SEARCH CONSULTANTS

At present there are only two accredited search consultants in Canada. If you are dealing with individuals purporting to be consultants, make sure they are licensed. The following are professionals licensed by Independent Search Consultants; they have followed a certification course: Joan Marshall, 63 Holborn Avenue, Nepean, Ontario K2C 3H1 (613-825-1640); Joan Lepp, Adoption Connection, Box 1674, Brandon, Manitoba R7A 6S3.

III. LIBRARIES AND ARCHIVES

As mentioned in the text of this book, city directories and telephone directories can be most useful. Your community may have these on file, or they will be in your local library. Provincial archives will also have them on file for your province.

Wills are also located at provincial archives. For years after 1900, they are to be found at the local county surrogate court offices. The Ontario Archives has on microfilm a copy of the index of all wills probated in Ontario since 1859 up to 1923. They will direct inquiries about wills to the appropriate surrogate court.

Land Assessment records may contain useful data such as the age, occupation and religious affiliation of the head of a household as well as the number of persons in the household. Assessment records are usually found at the local municipal office for the township, village, town or city, or in various archives.

Land records and township papers are also available.

Address: Ontario Archives, 77 Grenville Street, Queen's Park, Toronto, Ontario M7A 2R9 (416-965-6882, government inquiries; 416-965-4030, general inquiries).

The National Library in Ottawa has the most complete collection of city, county and provincial directories in Canada. Address: National Library of Canada, 395 Wellington Street, Ottawa, Ontario K1A 0N3.

The National Archives has a wealth of documents relating to genealogical searches. The address is the same as that of the National Library with the exception of the postal code, which is K1A 0N4. Census records are to be found here. In Ontario these records begin in 1842. There has been a census every ten years since 1851 where each member of a household is listed along with their age, occupation, country or province of birth and religious affiliation. These records are released for public use after 100 years.

If you have access to a university library, there are usually provisions for members of the public to use their inter-library loan facilities. It may also have a collection of major newspapers on microfiche.

Many major Canadian cities will have a research library in their system which will provide many of these services.

IV. GOVERNMENT SERVICES

A. REGISTRAR GENERAL

The depository of all records pertaining to births, marriages, deaths. In Ontario there has been a continuous record since 1869. Address: Registrar General of Ontario, Macdonald Block, Parliament Buildings, Toronto, Ontario M7A 1Y5.

B. DEPARTMENT OF NATIONAL DEFENCE

All military records. Address: National Personnel Records Centre, Public Archives Canada, Tunny's Pasture, Ottawa, Ontario K1A 0N3.

If you have reason to believe that the person for whom you are searching may have served in the British Forces, contact: Ministry of Defence, Army Records Centre, Bourne Avenue, Hayes, Middlesex, England UB3 1RF.

C. EMPLOYMENT AND IMMIGRATION CANADA

If you have data about the immigration of your family to Canada it is possible to trace them from these records. If you lack the data for Employment and Immigration to make a search, make an appointment to use the records yourself. Address: Query Response Centre, Employment and Immigration Canada, Ottawa, Ontario K1A 0J9 (613-994-4396).

D. DIVORCE RECORDS
If you know that there has been a divorce in the family, these records are available, but again, difficult to track down. The addresses of local registry offices may be obtained by writing: The Senate of Canada, Room 146-N, Centre Block, Parliament Buildings, Ottawa, Ontario K1A 0A4 (613-992-6943).

V. GENEALOGICAL SOURCES
A. TOMBSTONE INSCRIPTIONS:

An increasing number of pre-1900 tombstone inscriptions throughout Ontario are being transcribed and indexed. The most complete information may be obtained through: The Ontario Genealogical Society, Box 66, Station Q, Toronto, Ontario M4T 2L7, and/or the local county branch of OGS.

B. CENSUS

C. LAND RECORDS

These records and many others previously mentioned above and within the text can be used to trace a family. The Genealogical Research Library in London, Ontario, has some of its data open for public use and provides a service (at a fee) for searching specific records in Ontario, other parts of Canada, United States and Great Britain. Address: The Genealogical Research Library, Centennial House, 520 Wellington Street, London, Ontario N6A 3P9 (519-438-1456). They also have a booklet available that gives many useful hints as well as describing their services.

You might also wish to contact: The Church of Jesus Christ

of the Latter Day Saints, Genealogical Department, 50 East North Temple Street, Salt Lake City, Utah 84150.

VI. CHURCH RECORDS

Individual churches also keep their records of births, marriages, deaths, membership, etc. Try to identify the denomination of the person for whom you are searching; the archives of a local church in that denomination may be most useful. These may be somewhat difficult to track down for there is no consistency as to when information is transferred to central offices. Your local church should be able to give you the address of its national and/or provincial archives.

VII. SCHOOL RECORDS

Once you have located the area of the family for whom you are searching, it is possible to go through old school yearbooks and school registration records. University alumni offices are often willing to check their records to verify a name or to forward letters.

The Archives of Ontario have school records from that province from 1815 until 1976. Records older than thirty years are in most cases open for public research. Generally speaking, permission to consult records less than thirty years old must be obtained from the Ministry of Education.

The Central Records Department (not Archives) of the Toronto City Hall (other cities likely also have such departments) has a listing of school support taxes filed by year, name and address and cross-referenced to the Assessment Rolls.

VIII. NEWSPAPERS AND JOURNALS
A. BIRTHS, MARRIAGES, DEATHS

Major newspapers are on microfiche and are available through inter-library loan or at many large libraries or university libraries. The newspaper collection of the Ontario Archives specializes in newspapers published within the province from 1792 to 1930. The collection includes some 2,000 different mastheads, about 1,300 of which originate from the province.

B. ADVERTISEMENTS
Personal advertisements are certainly a long shot, but they have been known to work. Choose a significant date (birthday, Mother's Day, Christmas) to place your search ad. Community newspaper associations, covering all or several provinces, will place a single ad in all their member papers. Contact your local newspaper for more detailed information relating to this service in your area.

C. PROFESSIONAL JOURNALS
If you have identified a profession, place a classified advertisement in the appropriate journal.

D. MILITARY MAGAZINES
Legion has a large personal advertising section.

IX. INTERNATIONAL
- Registrar General, New Register House, Princess Street, Edinburgh, Scotland EH1 3YT.
- Registrar General, New Register Office, 49 Chichester Street, Belfast, Northern Ireland BT1 4H1.
- Registrar General's Office, Custom House, Dublin, Republic of Ireland.
- Registrar General, St. Catherine's House, 10 Kingsway, London, England WC2B 6JP.
- Association of British Adoption and Fostering Agents, 4 Southampton Road, London, England WC1B 4AA.
- Public Record Office, Chancery Lane, London, England W.C.2.
- The Librarian, National Library of Wales, Aberystwyth, Dyfed, SY23 3BU.

There will always be controversy but I sincerely believe that it is only a matter of time before the records will be fully open. In a sense the problem will die out as those of us who were adopted before the 1970s leave this world, for modern adoptions do provide the information and the facilities for information and contact to pass between the three principals in the adoption process. That still leaves a great number of years and a great number of people who are trapped in the process as it stands now. We will cope with the situation as best we can, but we cannot cease the struggle against the foundation of "dishonesty, exploitation and denial" upon which adoption rests (A.D. Sorosky et al., *The Adoption Triangle*). As Coleman Cox has put it, "Even the woodpecker owes his success to the fact that he uses his head and keeps pecking away until he finishes the job he starts."

Appendix III

PROVINCIAL INFORMATION

E ACH CANADIAN PROVINCE and territory has its own legislation and policies regarding adoption disclosure, non-identifying information, adoption orders, relinquishment documents, inheritance and gifts. In the 1980s social workers and legislators across the country became increasingly convinced of the need for a system that would give adoptees, birth parents, birth grandparents and other blood relatives access to information about their missing relatives.

There are, however, great differences between the provinces, and it is only by knowing the law and your rights that you will have any hope of success in your search. Insist on receiving the documentation you are entitled to, and if it is refused, carry your demand to the highest authority; and join (or found) an advocacy group.

Following is a brief outline of the present status of adoption disclosure registries and the availability of information in each province. For more detailed information, see Joan Marshall's *How to Search in Canada*, an extremely detailed and well researched book that not only includes the most up-to-date description of the registries but also gives examples of the forms necessary for application. Addresses of social service and child welfare offices are given where appropriate, as well as much other pertinent information. Copies may be obtained by writing to Searchline, 63 Holborn Avenue, Nepean, Ontario K2C 3H1; or by calling 613-825-1640.

NEWFOUNDLAND AND LABRADOR

Local Authority
Co-ordinator of Post Adoption Services
Department of Social Services
P.O. Box 4750
St. John's, Newfoundland A1C 5T7
(709-729-2662)

Status of Adoption Laws
Bill 52, An Act to Amend the Adoption of Children Act, 1972, was passed in 1990 and makes provision for release of identifying information when permission is given by the parties concerned.

Newfoundland and Labrador have a passive registry available to adoptees nineteen years of age and over, birth parents and adult siblings. The representative to whom I spoke explained that private searches in Newfoundland are relatively easy because of the geographical and social characteristics of the island. Closed adoption was in practice before 1949.

Non-identifying information is available on request as is the adoption order. There is no fee for any of these services.

PRINCE EDWARD ISLAND

Local Authority
The Director of Child Welfare
Department of Health & Social Services
Box 2000
Charlottetown, P.E.I. C1A 7N8
(902-368-5330)

Status of Adoption Laws and Services

Prince Edward Island, due to staff restrictions, does not have an official adoption disclosure and reunion service. When time allows, the provincial adoption co-ordinator does try to provide non-identifying information to adoptees, adoptive parents and medical professionals, and will often confirm information.

Since 1981 they have provided an *unofficial* passive registry "on which we record the names of all individuals expressing an interest in reunions. This was begun in anticipation of new legislative changes. Currently we are drafting a new Adoption Act which would allow for an official registry, the possibility of reunions and search. I would foresee counselling as being a part of this service" (from letter from Virginia J. MacEachern, MSW). The bill was tabled in 1990 but has progressed no further.

Legislative steps are being taken in the province and draft legislation includes the organization of an active register and counselling services to follow search-and-reunion.

There is a Parent Finders organization in P.E.I.: Parent Finders, c/o Margaret Bakker, R.R. #2, North Wiltshire, P.E.I. C0A 1Y0.

Background information is available, on written request, to adult adoptees eighteen years and older. There is no procedure to obtain adoption orders or relinquishment documents.

NOVA SCOTIA

Local Authority
Director, Family and Children's Services
Department of Community Services
Box 696
Halifax, Nova Scotia B3J 2T7
(902-424-2755)

Status of Laws and Services

Nova Scotia provides a passive registry for adult adoptees (over the age of nineteen) adopted before 1984, and birth parents. A discreet inquiry will be initiated only under the following circumstances for adoption orders granted before January 1, 1984:

• pressing medical or psychiatric need
• where the adoptee was legitimate at the time of the adoption
• where the birth parents married after the birth of the child
• where the birth parents lived in a common-law relationship

For adoptions after January 1, 1984, inquiries will be made on behalf of the adult adoptee after a one-year waiting period from date of the request. The waiting period may be waived under the following circumstances:

• medical or psychiatric need
• where the adoptee was legitimate at the time of the adoption
• where there is the possibility that the birth parent(s) may not live until the one-year waiting period is over

Non-identifying information is available to adult adoptees and birth parents. The adoption order is not available to the adoptee except through the adoptive family. A court order is necessary.

The statistics from this province are interesting. For the twelve-month period from April 1, 1988, to March 31, 1989, there were 322 inquiries about the disclosure service, 53 percent from adoptees, 26 percent from birth parents, 9 percent from adoptive parents and 8 percent from birth siblings. Of the 322 inquiries studied, 264 requested that their names be placed on the passive reunion registry. There have been a total of 26 reunions, 15 of these from mutual registrations. The remainder were as a result of an active search.

NEW BRUNSWICK

Local Authority
Post Adoption Record Disclosure Services
Department of Social Services
P.O. Box 6000
Fredericton, N.B. E3B 5H1
(506-453-2949)

Status of Laws and Services
The leaflet from New Brunswick is well-organized, well-thought-out and sensitive. It deals with the concerns and worries of all parties in a few very well-chosen words. The registry, created in 1981, is now semi-active for adult adoptees nineteen and over. If the name of the birth parents is not listed, you may request the department to make a search for birth parents or an adult sibling. Pre-reunion counselling is available to both parties. No identifying information is released unless both adoptee and birth parents have consented in writing.

Non-identifying information is available, as is the adoption order (if you know your birth surname). There is no charge for any of these services.

QUEBEC

Local Authorities
The Adoption Secretariat
3700 Berri Street
Montreal, Quebec H2L 4G9
(514-873-5226)
Ville Marie Social Service Centre
4515 Rene Levesque Boulevard West
Montreal, Quebec H3Z 1R9
(514-989-1885)

Status of Laws and Services
Joan Marshall, in her book *How to Search in Canada*, expresses
the Quebec situation most succinctly when she says: "Quebec
is ever-changing and has no concrete guidelines. At one time
it had the most progressive adoption disclosure service in
Canada, but that situation has now deteriorated badly. In
short, if your adoption was legalized in the province of Quebec, your search will be a *frustrating, time consuming*, perhaps
even a *dehumanizing* experience, but it is possible, and the most
important word to remember and to continually remember, is
that it is POSSIBLE."

In Quebec, each social service department is responsible
for its own records. Note that since 1979 there have been no
recognized private adoptions. In 1978 the provincial government granted permission to facilitate reunions to the
Centre de Services Sociaux Montreal-Metropolitain, but for
some reason did not grant the same right to other social
services agencies in the province. This was an active service.
There are now fourteen social service centres that are man-
dated by the government to provide social services, including adoption services. All English adoptions that took place
in Montreal are handled by the Ville Marie Social Service
Centre.

The Quebec Civil Code, October, 1985, declares confidential
the judicial and administrative files respecting the adoption of
a child. The court may allow an adoption file to be examined
for the purpose of study, teaching, research or a public inquiry,
provided that the anonymity of the child, the parents and the
adopter is preserved. This is a very interesting possible loophole.

Once a person has reached the age of majority he is entitled
to information in his file that will enable him to find his
biological parents and vice versa, but only if the parties have
previously consented. The law provides that such consent
"must not be solicited" (Art. 632 C.C.Q.). The courts have

interpreted "solicitation" in two different ways. In one set of cases the courts hold that this article contains a prohibition against contacting the biological parents or notifying them that their child desires to get in touch with them unless the parents had given their consent to such an inquiry prior to the adopted person's request. The other group of cases followed the decision of the Court of Appeal in Guy vs. Centre de Services Sociaux du Quebec (1984) C.A. 526; it is now accepted in Quebec that even without their prior consent, the Centre for Social Services can contact adopted persons or biological parents in order to inform them about the intentions of, respectively, their parents or children to trace their families or children. The centre will only act as an intermediary and no court will force it to exercise pressure on one of the parties to contact the other party. However, if the centre refuses to act, the court can order it to make the necessary inquiries and make a report within a reasonable delay. In such a case a motion has to be made to the youth court at the domicile of the adopted person or of the biological parents.

Cutbacks in the social services budgets have resulted in waiting lists so long that one could wait virtually forever. A recent interview with a member of a finders' group in Quebec revealed that, in one city, one social worker has been appointed to respond to searching adoptees. She works alone, has been given only one day a week to spend on this task, and has a waiting list of 1,500 individuals who want information.

Application must be made to the agency that handled the adoption. Policy varies from agency to agency. Remember that the right to receive non-identifying information exists in law (Youth Protection Act, section 131.1). In most cases there is no fee for this service.

Adoption orders are available from the court that dealt with the adoption. Only rarely does the birth name appear on this document.

ONTARIO

Local Authority
Ministry of Community and Social Services
Operational Coordination Branch
Adoption Unit
2nd floor - 700 Bay Street
Toronto, Ontario M5G 1E9
(416-963-0709; toll free in Ontario: 1-800-387-5477)

Status of Laws and Services
Anyone involved in a search that touches on the province of Ontario should make a point of obtaining an excellent free booklet from the ministry: "Adoption Disclosure Services."

Ontario legislation has undergone great changes in the past decade, not only in its laws, but also in its facilities for searching adoptees. (See Appendix IV for background information to these developments.)

THE ADOPTION DISCLOSURE REGISTRY: Briefly stated:
- any adoptee over the age of eighteen, or an adoptive parent on behalf of their child, or a birth relative may register with the ADR and apply for non-identifying information. (This should first be done through the Children's Aid Society that arranged the adoption. If this is not known, contact the Adoption Unit.)
- If a match is made, or if a birth relative is located, each party must meet with a staff member.
- Both parties must agree to release of the identifying information; if this occurs, counselling follows.
- Reunion is up to the people involved. The counsellor is available to act as a go-between in making arrangements.
- The process may be stopped at any point by either party.
- If a match is not made, the adoptee may request a confidential search. This service is not available to birth parents.

The Adoption Unit will guide you through the process of inquiry, beginning with helping to find the Children's Aid through which you were adopted, or determining whether the process was handled through a lawyer. ADOPTION ORDER: The adoption order is available *only* if you know your birth name. Adoptive parents can get it without birth name.

NON-IDENTIFYING INFORMATION: Available for those over eighteen years of age, and to minors with their adoptive parents' consent. In most cases, non-identifying information is available through the Children's Aid Society branch that handled the adoption.

As of March, 1990, there are 12,765 adoptees and 7,491 birth parents registered, for a total of 20,256 applicants. Ontario has started a two-year program to reduce the backlog and the ministry's staff now numbers 52, up from 25 in 1989.

The Children's Aid has also had to cope with an enormous backlog, which is expected to be reduced to "manageable proportions" by the end of 1991. In the six months from January to June 1990 it was reduced to two years (down from three years as of October, 1989). The number of open cases at the Children's Aid of Metropolitan Toronto presently stands at 1,100.

MANITOBA

Local Authority
Family Services
Post-Adoption Registry
2nd floor
114 Garry Street
Winnipeg, Manitoba R3C 1G1
(204-945-6962; toll free in Manitoba: 1-800-282-8060)

Status of Laws and Services
The Post-Adoption Service began in 1981 as a passive registry

for birth parents, adopted adults and adoptive parents on behalf of a minor child. On April 1, 1986, legislation permitted registrations by adult biological siblings as well as a search on behalf of registered adult adoptees for both parents and/or any adult biological siblings not placed for adoption.

Manitoba has a very clear brochure, information from which is reproduced here by permission of the department. Manitoba's is a passive registry, but will initiate searches under certain circumstances. It will *not* search for birth siblings who are adopted or search for birth siblings who have not reached the age of eighteen years.

Adopted adults (over eighteen), birth parents and adult siblings of adult adoptees, and adoptive parents may register. Adopted adults, birth parents and adult birth siblings may register at any time. Adoptive parents of minors may, on behalf of the child, register when the child is under the age of eighteen. However, once the adopted child becomes an adult, the adoptive parents may register only with the child's consent, and only on the child's behalf.

Counselling is available, and each party must be involved in at least one counselling session before a meeting takes place. The agency will arrange a meeting with consent of all concerned. Counselling is also available for adoptive parents.

Non-identifying information is available, as is the adoption order. The adoption order does not show the birth name. There is no cost for any of these services.

In the period from 1981 to 1988 a total of 3,582 persons registered with the Adoption Register: 1,855 adoptees, 1,462 birth parents, 106 adoptive parents, and 159 siblings. In this period there were 240 matches.

SASKATCHEWAN

Local Authority
Saskatchewan Social Services

Provincial Adoption Registry
2240 Albert Street
Regina, Saskatchewan S4P 3V7
(306-787-3654; toll free in Saskatchewan: 1-800-667-7539)

Status of Laws and Services
Saskatchewan's Post-Adoption Registry was established in 1982. It is active for adopted adults eighteen years and over. "Through discreet inquiries the Registry determines if the birth parent is agreeable to contact with the adoptee. Identifying information is released only on consent of both parties." Adoptive parents may get information for their children if they are under eighteen, and may facilitate a reunion.

Non-identifying information is available, as is the adoption order.

Fees are charged by the Post-Adoption Registry for services provided. Fees as of October 1990:
- Non-identifying background document $60
- Copy of document $35
- Registration and Active Search $35
- Search and contact $265
- Contact by Mutual Request $180
- Search and contact with second and subsequent family member(s) $180

There are circumstances where these fees will be waived or modified.

ALBERTA

Local Authority
Post-Adoption Registry
12th floor
Seventh Street Plaza
South Tower
10030 - 107 Street

Edmonton, Alberta T5J 3E7
(403-427-6387; toll free in Alberta: Contact the RITE operator
nearest you through a regular long-distance operator if you
do not have RITE service in your area.)

Status of Laws and Services
Alberta is in the process of revising its post-adoption services,
but for the present it operates as a passive registry, as it has done
since 1985. It is estimated that there have been 80,000 adoptions
in Alberta from 1919 to the end of 1989. Adopted adults over the
age of eighteen who were adopted in Alberta, birth parents and
adult siblings may register. Counselling given on request.

Non-identifying information and the adoption order are
available. For adoptions registered before July 1, 1966, the
birth name may appear; it will not appear for adoptions after
this date. There is no charge for any of these services.

BRITISH COLUMBIA

Local Authorities
Ministry of Health
818 Fort Street
Victoria, B.C. V8W 1H8
(604-387-4834)

Ministry of Health
Division of Vital Statistics
Vancouver Regional Office
800 Hornby Street (Robson Square)
Vancouver, B.C. V6Z 2C5
(604-660-2937)

Ministry of Health
Division of Vital Statistics
#203 - 126 East 15th Street

North Vancouver, B.C. V7L 2P9
(604-660-1268)

Status of Laws and Services
British Columbia's Adoption Reunion Registry was established in 1987 and is passive. Persons nineteen years of age or older who were adopted in British Columbia and natural parents may register. The registry does not provide information about biological brothers or sisters, instigate any form of search or provide counselling before a reunion. There is a fee of $25 and the application must be witnessed.

If a match is made, each party is sent the name, address and telephone number of the other. It is then up to the individuals whether or not to arrange contact.

The most recent statistics are as of June 1990. To this date there have been 1,628 applicants and 73 matches.

Non-identifying information is available "in certain instances." To apply for this, write to the Hornby Street address above. There is no fee for this service or for the adoption order. To obtain the adoption order write to: Direct Services Unit - Post Adoption, Family and Children's Services Division, Ministry of Social Services and Housing, Parliament Buildings, Victoria, B.C. V8W 3A2.

This is only available if granted *after* 1968. Before this date, only a confirmation of adoption will be given.

YUKON

Local Authority
Adoption Disclosure Registry
Health and Human Resources
#201 - Royal Bank Building
4114 4th Avenue
Whitehorse, Yukon Y1A 2C6
(403-667-3002)

Status of Laws and Services
The information provided by the Yukon is interesting. As well as their brochure, they also have separate sheets titled "Some Considerations for Adoptees" and "Some Considerations for Birth Parents."

The Yukon has a passive registry, which was established in 1985 and is open to adult adoptees nineteen or older, birth parents, birth siblings and birth grandparents. A confidential search can be requested by the adoptee for pertinent medical data. The department will assist in an exchange of letters, telephone conversations, and if both parties wish, with a personal reunion.

Non-identifying information is available as is a copy of the adoption order. There is no charge for any of these services.

NORTHWEST TERRITORIES

Local Authority
Family and Children's Services
Department of Social Services
P.O. Box 1320
Yellowknife, NWT X1A 2L9
(403-873-7943)

Status of Laws and Services
The Northwest Territories has no legislation directly relating to adoption disclosure, and no registry exists. The department does, however, recognize the need for exchange of information, and they will give information to adult adoptees nineteen and older and birth parents if there is mutual consent, and will facilitate reunions unofficially. The adoptive parents must also agree. Counselling is available but not mandatory.

Non-identifying information is available to adult adoptees and birth relatives. The adoption order is also available to adoptees only but will not show birth surname.

There is no charge for any of these services.

Appendix IV

OPEN RECORDS — A CLOSER LOOK AT ONTARIO

U NTIL RECENTLY, ONTARIO adoption law closely followed that of Great Britain. However, we are now far behind the British Isles in acceptance of the principle of open records. They permit access to original birth certificates, and have done so since 1976.

Before the First World War, adoptions were a private matter. There were no laws governing the passing of children from one family to another, for whatever reason. The first Child Protection Act in Canada was passed in Ontario in 1893, but there was no specific mention of the adoption of children. The administration of the law was placed in the hands of the Children's Aid Society (founded in 1891); the society's continued, present-day involvement in adoption stems from its original mandate to care for neglected children. There was not at that time any *legal* question of secrecy, of changing information on birth certificates, or any other of the legal games that now accompany adoption. The first Adoption Act in Ontario (1921) made no mention of secret documents or sealed records. The second Adoption Act (1927), however, introduced severe restrictions on the disclosure of information; for the first time all records were sealed. There is nothing in the legislative debates of the time that would indicate why this change was made, but the belief that secrecy was appropriate seems to have been common at the time: a similar act was passed in England in 1926. These restrictions were also reflected in legislation in the United States, Scotland and Australia.

The post-war period was a time of enormous change in Canada. On the one hand Victorian morality was still strong, but on the other, there was the obvious difficulty of what to do with illegitimate children. Unmarried parenthood still carried a stigma and this extended to the child. Adoption could not erase it, but it might hide it. It has been suggested that

> ... the initiation of closed records resulted from the concerns of child placement workers whose primary intentions were to protect the child against blackmail from extended family members, to avoid the stigma of illegitimacy. ... *The records were not sealed to protect the birth parents, nor did they occur for demands made on behalf of adoptive parents as was often assumed.*[1]

If these considerations were the reason behind the law, surely the records may now be opened. Is this a case of a law remaining on the books for reasons totally different from those for which it was promulgated?

This conspiracy of silence has led to today's fundamental problem: the conflict between the spirit of the Canadian Charter of Rights and Freedoms and the historical understanding between social workers and adoptive and birth parents that the children involved should never know the whole truth. Somewhere, the needs of the adoptees, the birth children, have become lost. It is a matter now of "the right of the adult adoptee to know against the right of the birth mother to confidentiality. But a close look at the lobby groups reveals that it is the conservative adoption agencies and adoptive parents, not the birth mothers, who are struggling to keep records closed."[2] In actual fact, of the several thousand birth parents who were surveyed by Concerned United Birth Parents, only *four* did not want to make contact.[3] At the moment the legislators, to various degrees, deny that a problem exists.

Over and over again we read of birth mothers who feel they were coerced into giving up their babies. Silverman, Campbell, Patti and Style recently studied 170 reunions between birth parents and adoptees. In 79 percent of them the birth parents initiated the search for their children.[4] "The birth parents who searched were more likely to have received counselling that supported surrendering their children; many felt coerced into agreeing they 'could/should not keep the baby.'"[5]

This is changing, for since the late 1960s social agencies have been "careful to indicate to unmarried mothers that they may have some resources to rely upon if they choose to keep their children, and that they should consider the options of either keeping or relinquishing their child."[6]

Hand in hand with the question of sealed records is the question of what is contained in those records. Between 1921, when the first Act was passed, and 1979 there was was no requirement for *any* information about the birth family to follow the child into his or her new life. The only report left in the file with the ministry was that made by the local Children's Aid, on the adoptive family, to satisfy the ministry's provisions. Now, however, the Children's Aid must keep records on the birth family as well. It has only been since 1979 that the ministry records have included such basic general background information as the nationality, education and medical histories of birth parents.

The Hurst Report in 1954 was the first official recognition that the situation had a number of troubling aspects and that certain realities were not being taken sufficiently into consideration, in fact

. . . that adopted people did develop a curiosity about their backgrounds; such curiosity was not to be taken as a symptom of neurosis but as perfectly natural; there were, accordingly, benefits from providing this information; these benefits had to do with the person's psychological well-being, curiosity and "needs" as opposed to material interest in inheritance. . . . A number of witnesses in England thought that the adopted person has a right to this information (birth information) and expressed the view that it is not in the interests of adopted children to be permanently precluded from satisfying their natural curiosity.[7]

Non-identifying information has always been given out by the Toronto Children's Aid Society. Before the late 1970s it was given verbally through appointment with a social worker, but after 1979, because of the increasing number of requests for this information, all inquiries have been handled by mail. The content included depended on the agency.

An important step towards enlightened change in the laws of Ontario came in 1978 when the Child Welfare Act was amended to introduce a voluntary disclosure registry. This was a passive registry: no search was instigated at any point, and so relatively few matches were made. If a match was made, the three parties to adoption — the birth parent, the adoptive parent and the adoptee — all had to agree to disclosure before a reunion was arranged or identifying information released.

However, there was a time-bomb hidden in this amendment to the Act. The writers had not thought of defining the different types of information that might be given, nor did they provide any criteria for the release of information, however defined. The bomb was detonated in 1980 by Judge Killeen in a judgement relating to an adult adoptee's request for her records. Elizabeth Ferguson had applied to the VDR and when a match was not made she approached the courts. The court ruled against her application on the basis that her need to know was not great enough. (Ferguson v. the Director of Child Welfare [1983]). The judge, in his comments, criticized the Child Welfare Act for the omission of a definition of information and the criteria for its release, because the legislation contained no comment of any kind applying to any sort of release. The judge went on to state that until the law was changed "he had no basis for deciding what information could be released."[8] The Ontario Court of Appeal refused to consider the provisions of the Canadian Constitution as articulated in the Charter of Rights and Freedoms since they were not to go into effect until 1985. This effectively sealed the Voluntary Disclosure Registry and suspended the legislation that had permitted it. In the absence of the amendment it was illegal for anyone to disclose any information. The ministry advised the Children's Aid Societies that it would no longer release adoption information from the ministry files except through the registry, which required three-party consent. It advised the Children's Aid Societies to consult their own lawyers before continuing the practice of releasing non-identifying information; consequently many Children's Aid Societies closed their information departments. Some of the larger centres continued to give information (e.g., London, Ottawa and Toronto).

In November, 1983, the ministry published "The Child and Family Services Act: Draft Legislation and background paper." The decision on post-adoption access to information was stated as follows: "The recommendation that the court on making an adoption order not be permitted to grant post-adoption access to the child was overwhelmingly supported, and has been incorporated into the draft legislation."[9]

One must question the basis on which this decision was made, for when Dr. Ralph Garber, dean of the Faculty of Social Work at the University of Toronto, made a search of "background papers and provincial government documents that spoke to the questions of adoption disclosure, it was expected that . . . information would have been available to inform the Legislature and the Cabinet leading to their decision to restrict access to adoption information. In fact no papers could be found that spoke to that side of the question. To the contrary the background papers commissioned by the ministry over the past ten years indicated the opposite — that greater disclosure was necessary."[10]

Very interesting! Apart from the timing, which suggested that we followed the 1926 example of Great Britain, there is nothing in the record at all to indicate why Canada chose then, or in future legislation, to implement a sealed-record policy. Is it possible that a small committee of non-qualified and perhaps biased members of Parliament made this decision, which has affected so many thousands of adoptees for so many years? Yet the legislation of 1983 was based on the premise of the previous law.

This background paper slid over the question of adoption information disclosure by commenting that the process of consultation "has been used by numerous groups and individuals as an opportunity for presenting their view that access to adoption information should be made easier. The draft legislation DOES NOT change the existing law on this issue."[11]

Section 148 says clearly that "the court shall not make an order for access to the child by a birth parent or a member of the birth parent's family." Section 156 (2) continues: "The documents used upon an application for an adoption order shall be sealed up and filed in the office of the court by the proper officer of the court and shall not be open for inspection except upon an order of the court or the written direction of a Director."[12]

The Ontario government is clearly aware, and aware to the degree that they make a point of it in a policy statement, that there were a number of adoptees who cared so much, whose need to know was so strong, that they would go to any lengths, including using non-identifying information as the basis of years-long searches, to find their families.

> While there is general support for increased access to non-identifying information, there is an issue of how to prevent the bringing together of a number of pieces of otherwise non-identifying information in a way that could lead to the identification of an individual. . . . It is impossible, of course, to guarantee that access to non-identifying information will never lead to an individual's identification. (The truth of this has been demonstrated by determined adoptees and parent finder groups who effect reunions today despite restrictive disclosure laws.)[13]

Nevertheless, the government believed that the risk of inadvertent disclosure could be minimized by the introduction of regulations and guidelines designed to address the problem.

In 1984, Bill 77 (entitled "An Act Respecting the Protection and Well-being of Children and their Families") replaced the Child Welfare Act of 1978. All appeals against the old disclosure provisions, especially against requiring the adoptive parents' consent for the Adoption Disclosure Registry to give information to *adult* adoptees, were totally ignored in this new legislation. Section 157 of this bill specifically forbade the disclosure of *any* information except through the Adoption Disclosure Registry and in fact increased the restrictiveness of the legislation by stating, in subsection 10, that "no person shall inspect, remove, disclose, alter or permit the inspection, removal, disclosure or alteration of information kept in the register, except with the Director's written authority."

A former executive director of the Children's Aid Society of Metropolitan Toronto observed, "If the adoption section of Bill 77 is passed, we shall be witnessing a human tragedy of significant proportion. Quite simply, the government proposes to disenfranchise thousands of adults in this province who were once adopted children."[14]

Because of public concern about the restrictive nature of section 157, which also cast doubt on the legality of sharing *non-identifying* information, section 157 was *not included* in the final legislation, which was passed in December, 1984, and became effective November 1, 1985. Section 157 was delayed indefinitely. Had this section been included Ontario would have become the only province in Canada with such a restriction.

In the spring of 1985, partially as a result of the furor that had arisen over the results of the Ferguson case and the subsequent debate over section 157, Dr. Robert Elgie, the new minister of community and social services, took action. He asked Dr. Ralph Garber of the University of Toronto to act as special commissioner to investigate the disclosure of adoption information and to address himself to the whole question of identifying and non-identifying information and its accessibility.

This report was published in November, 1985. Although open hearings were not conducted because of the limited time frame in which Dr. Garber had to produce the report, he received many submissions and petitions. His overall observation was that there is a very strong feeling in Ontario that more information should be available to adoptees. He observed, "The citizens of Ontario are not known to be reticent about expressing their opinions at public inquiries. The almost total absence of letters or submissions from those opposed to disclosure suggests that the opposition to disclosure is muted or very limited, since they have had ample opportunity to express their opinions and did not choose to do so. A poll, limited to viewers of TV Ontario's 'Speaking Out' program of October 31, 1985, on adoption disclosure, called in at a rate of 9 to 1 in favour of disclosure of birth records."[15]

He recognized a fundamental principle when he states that "the principle with respect to birth parents is that the renunciation of a right to parent their child at an earlier stage in their lives does not limit their right to reconsider their relationship with their adult child, at a later stage."[16]

Ralph Garber's recommendations included:

> The adoptee who has attained adult status should be accorded the same benefits and responsibilities as other adults, including access to his original statement of live birth should he desire it. He should not be required to have "parental consent" to access this information. . . . That the Child and Family Services Act be amended to permit the release of identifying information through the Disclosure Register, and accompanied by mandatory interpretive counselling to adult adoptees (18 and over) . . . but released in stages with interpretive counselling, beginning with release of the adoption order and the original long form birth certificate."[17]

To release this information to the adoptee without permission of the adoptive parents or the consent of those whose identity was to be disclosed, however, required "the consent of the persons to be contacted."[18] Dr. Garber also recommended

> . . . that the Adoption Disclosure Register shall undertake a reasonable and discreet search of up to nine months for those not registered and act as an intermediary between the person requesting information or contact and the person(s) from whom it is sought.[19]

Dr. Garber stated that "the first principle with respect to the facts surrounding an individual's adoption is that those facts belong to that person regardless of where and how they are safeguarded. Facts about adoption should be restored to a person if they have been removed or hidden, regardless of what interpretation may be made concerning these facts."[20] This conclusion from a scholar in his position was most positive. Unfortunately, the Ontario government was not prepared to go quite so far; in his reply to the report the minister recognizes that adopted persons indeed have a "need and a right to information about their biological roots" and that the government "has a responsibility to assist adult adoptees who are seeking identifying information or reunion with birth relatives."[21] But the government "thinks Dr. Garber's proposals go too far in shifting the control over adoption information to adoptees and away from birth parents. Such a shift seems particularly controversial and problematic when applied retroactively, as Dr. Garber has recommended."[22]

The conclusions of this reply to the Garber report recommend that:

- adoptive parents have access to all identifying information about their child.
- adult adoptees have access to all available non-identifying information about their birth families.
- adult adoptees also have access to identifying information with the consent of their birth parents.
- adult adoptees have assistance and counselling from the Adoption Disclosure Registry or Children's Aid Society in obtaining the consents and in arranging a reunion.
- birth parents, adult birth siblings and birth grandparents may register in the Adoption Disclosure Registry and receive identifying information with permission of the adult adoptee.
- Children's Aid Societies and licensees are to release non-identifying information to those who are eligible who request it. Efforts are also to be made to keep updated files on the adoptee and birth families.
- the mandate of the Adoption Disclosure Registry is to be

expanded to "include public education about adoption disclosure, post-adoption counselling services for registrants and other affected by disclosure, and search activities on behalf of adult adoptees."[23]

• provision is also to be made for the Ministry to release information which is required to protect the health, safety or welfare of any person.

This report is now available through the Ontario government, and anyone who is searching or interested in the question of adoption should obtain a copy. Along with his recommendations Dr. Garber also gives an overview of the facts and fallacies of adoption and of the history.

As a direct result of these preliminary studies many of the changes recommended were implemented by this legislation. The resulting legislation, "An Act to Amend the Children and Family Services Act, 1984, and certain other acts in relation to Adoption Disclosure" (Bill 165, Second session of the 33rd Legislature of The Province of Ontario), was proclaimed on July 6, 1987.

The most significant part of the law is the increased mandate of the Adoption Disclosure Registry. These changes indicate a broadening acceptance of adoption reunion and identification, but the problem with the Adoption Disclosure Registry is one of publicity. Although representatives appear on radio and television when the opportunity arises, and articles occasionally appear in newspapers, the dispensing of information on the registry is costly. Since the registry is a government department, the law states that any advertisement it places in newspapers must be put in every newspaper in the province.

The government now recognizes the importance of medical history, and provision has been made for release of information where "the situation is life-threatening, or otherwise very serious."[24] But what information would this be? It must be remembered that medical histories were not to be found in the ministry files before 1979. Any records in the Children's Aid files may easily be twenty or thirty years out of date. Is the government prepared to contact birth families of all searchers and compile up-to-date files? If not, then the offer to make "important" medical histories available is an empty one.

In the policy statement, "Ontario's New Adoption Disclosure Policy," the Minister of Community and Social Services, then Hon. John Sweeney, writes: "As Dr. Garber's report recommends, the ministry intends to *encourage (but not require)* adoption participants to update the information that adoption agencies and the ministry have on file. . . . Similarly, birth parents and adult adoptees would be *encouraged* to update their medical histories. . . ."[25]

We can only hope that the spirit of the Garber report will trickle down through the system. However, the frontpiece to the provincial government's reply is worthy of note — and concern. This was quoted from an article titled *"Adoption Workers' Views on Sealed Records"* printed in *Public Welfare*/Spring, 1986:

> A complex balance of different rights exists within every adoption. The rights of all parties in the adoption triangle must be considered and weighed — a task that is not easy. Ultimately, choice must be made regarding whose rights should supersede the rights of others. This means there will be times when some members of the adoption triangle are satisfied and others dissatisfied with the distribution of power. This dilemma cannot be avoided; thus, it is unlikely the sealed adoption controversy can ever be fully resolved.

The juxtaposition of this quote to the document, "Ontario's New Adoption Disclosure Policy," is disturbing. The concept of power has dangerous implications. This seems to confirm that there is indeed a power struggle involved in the question.

The conclusion that it is unlikely that there ever will come a time when the problem can be resolved is discouraging, especially since it was written by a social worker involved in adoption. Laws can be written, but the front-line soldiers — the social workers — must have the sensitivity to implement them in the true spirit of the need. We should have grave concerns about the openness of attitude when these people are still talking about power and rights being superseded, and not talking about human rights and psychological well-being.

The legislation has dealt with a number of important issues. It is not perfect, but it is a beginning. However, will it continue? With this act, hope has been given to all searching adoptees in Ontario. We are still at the mercy of our birth parents' agreeing to meet us, but no longer must we have the written permission of our adoptive parents. To this degree the law has recognized us as adults. Until this issue has been faced, the adoptee will still be treated as a special class, with special restrictions.

Notes
1. Ehrlich, *A Time to Search*, p.10.
2. Lifton, B.J., *Lost and Found*, p.264.
3. Giddens, *Faces of Adoption*, p.132.
4. Silverman, Campbell, Patti, Style: *Reunions between Adoptees and Birth Parents*, p.532.
5. Ibid., p.524.
6. Garber, R., *Disclosure of Adoption Information*, p.16.
7. Haimes, *Adoption and Social Policy*, pp.13, 14.
8. Garber, R., p.1.
9. "Child and Family Services Act," p.137.
10. Garber, R., pp.4, 5.
11. Ibid., p.138.
12. Ibid., p.155.
13. *Ontario's New Adoption Disclosure Policy*, p.2.
14. *Parent Finders Communique*, April, 1985.
15. Garber, R., p.3.

16. Ibid., p.26.
17. Ibid., p.41.
18. Ibid, p.43.
19. Ibid., p.46.
20. Ibid., p.27.
21. *Ontario's New Adoption Disclosure Policy*, p.5.
22. Ibid., p.5.
23. Ibid., p.15.
24. Adoption Disclosure Services Information document, p.11.
25. Ibid., p.11.

Appendix V

A LOOK INTO
HISTORY

The woman conceived and bore a son; and when she
saw that he was a goodly child, she hid him three
months. And when she could hide him no longer she
took for him a basket made of bulrushes . . . and she
put the child in it and placed it among the reeds at
the river's brink. . . . Now the daughter of Pharaoh
came down to bathe at the river, and her maidens
walked beside the river; she saw the basket among
the reeds and sent her maid to fetch it. When she
opened it she saw the child; and lo, the babe was
crying. She took pity on him. . . . And the child
grew . . . and became her son; and she named him
Moses.

Holy Bible, Exodus 2

THE RELATED ACTS of giving up children and the adoption of children go back into the dim records of history. Even in earliest times there was a need for rules affecting the relationship of the adopted person within the society. The Code of Hammurabi (a Babylonian king of the eighteenth century B.C.) stated that if an adoptee denied that his adoptive parents were his real parents his tongue was cut out and if an adoptee, "searched out, looked upon his father's house and tried to enter it, hating his adoptive father," he lost his eyes. Even then, almost four thousand years ago, some adoptees were searching! The Code of Hammurabi did recognize that there were extenuating circumstances and allowed that an adoptee who showed an "extraordinary longing for his natural parents" might rejoin them.[1] The code is about four thousand years ahead of the current legislation in Ontario, which states in no uncertain terms, in Section 151, "An adoption order under section 141 is final and irrevocable." Once this paper has been signed and is before the courts, any information relating to the child is sealed, never to resurface. At least our legislators draw the line at physical mutilation for those of us who wish to look upon our father's house!

We read of Romulus, who was cared for by a she-wolf and a woodpecker (and we think we may have been mismatched!). In biblical times Moses was dumped in the bullrushes to sail off to a greater future. Cases of adoption were very frequent among the Greeks and the Romans, and strictly regulated by law. In Athens the power of adoption was "allowed to all citizens who were of sound mind, and who possessed no male offspring of their own, and it could be exercised either during lifetime or by testament."[3] Here the purpose of adoption was to secure an heir so that the family line and inheritance could be passed on. Once in force the adoption could not be renounced and the children ceased to have any claim of kindred or inheritance through their natural father; interestingly, this did not apply to their natural mother. If the adopted son had a son, he could then (having supplied an heir for his adoptive family) return to his birth family — in this case the child remained with the grandfather's family and the connection was severed at the second generation. The motive for adoption in Rome was also to prevent a line from dying out and perpetuate the worship of ancestors. In most cases the father had to be past the point of there being a reasonable chance of him ever siring children and he had to be at least eighteen years older than the individual in question. The birth father formally and publicly "sold" his offspring to the adoptive father. Only citizens were adopted, so there was no question of adopting for the advantage of the child.

The *Encyclopedia Britannica* (9th edition, 1875-89) refers to the part played by the "legal fiction of adoption" in primitive societies. Henry S. Maine, author of *Ancient Law*, puts forward the theory that "had [adoption] never existed, primitive groups could not have coalesced except on terms of absolute superiority on one side, and absolute subjection on the other. With the institution of adoption, however, one people might *feign itself* as descended from the same stock" as the dominant peoples in the area and "amicable relations were thus established between stocks which, but for this expedient, must have submitted to the arbitrament of the sword with all its consequences."[3]

In Hindu law, as indeed as in most ancient societies, wills are almost unknown and adoption would take their place if there were no living offspring. It was preferable to adopt as close a relative as possible, and adoptions were kept within the same class, and if possible within the same village.

In pre-revolutionary China, an heir could be the offspring of a concubine, or a son-in-law could "become a son" by marrying the daughter of a family without a male heir in her home, so adoption in the traditional sense was not as common as in some ancestor-worship societies. However, sons were vitally important in a society which placed a strong emphasis on ancestor worship.

Adoption has never been an important factor in non-hereditary societies (Africa) and the Islamic religion forbids it.

In the west, throughout the Middle Ages and until the beginning of the nineteenth century there was no legislated adoption process. Children were placed as servants or apprentices or attached to families in the wealthier classes. It was not until the Napoleonic Code that the concept of regulations concerning adoption reappeared. England and Switzerland were the last countries in Europe to allow adoption.

As strict Victorian morality gave way to a more "modern" life, there was distinct "public alarm at the prospect of illegitimate children becoming a charge on the government or on charitable institutions."[4] Adoption was an important way of getting children off the charity rolls and it was recognized that it was far healthier for children to be brought up in a stable home environment than in an institution. Today, a framework is in place to make it possible for a single mother to raise a child but it must be remembered that at the time of these first Adoption Acts welfare, subsidized housing and family counselling were essentially non-existent.

Adoption in the Western world came to be seen as an act to save children — to relieve poor families of their burdens or to find homes for orphaned or abandoned children. It was also a way to relieve the taxpayer of the responsibility of caring for "the accidents of Fate" in institutions. The tragedy of many of these children who were shipped to farms in Australia or Canada at the turn of the century is well documented.

An attitude of suspicion surrounded adoption and it was seen as either a way to provide the mother with a cover for her "mistake" or a "misguided attempt to imitate nature."[5] Legislation came to reflect these suspicious attitudes on the part of those opposed to the concept of adoption.

On the other hand, these children had to be placed and as well as agencies private "baby stores" existed in the United States (and perhaps in Canada) complete with illustrated catalogues. An excerpt from one of these turn-of-the-century sales pitches reads:

Taken as a class, they are recognized as being far brighter than the average offered for adoption. They are more affectionate, have better dispositions and temperaments and have clearer heads and brighter intellects. The risks usual with adoption are decreased, and their attendant consequences diminished. . . . [6]

The *Encyclopedia Canadiana* of 1957 in its entry on adoption expresses most clearly the attitude of that time toward unmarried parenthood:

It used to be thought that the primary goal of service to unmarried parents was to redeem the mother and to see that her child was not neglected. The more modern concept, however, regards unmarried parents as troubled people who require counselling and assistance in order to solve their personal problems and to make a satisfactory plan for the child. Although many people still hold that the unmarried mother should be encouraged to care for her own child, either in her own home or in a foster home, there appears to be an increasing trend toward placing the child for adoption. [7]

The general attitude at this time was that a social worker had succeeded if most of his or her "clients" placed their children for adoption, and that they had failed if a woman kept her child.

We have become so complacent about modern medical care that we often forget the high mortality of the past. In the days before antibiotics, the simplest infection could result in death. Cemeteries are full of young women who died in childbirth, often leaving several young children. If the husband did not remarry forthwith these children would have to be cared for by others. Adoption in these early days was dealt with quietly in the community, or children were raised by a member of the extended family.

We take birth control for granted, but it was not so long ago that families of eight or ten or more children were relatively common. Frequently families simply could not afford to care for these children and other homes had to be found for them.

While legislation in all Canadian provinces sets out the conditions under which an adoption placement may be made, in no instance does it require that placements shall be made only by child welfare agencies. Many children were placed for adoption by natural parents or other persons acting on their behalf. Almost all the provinces now require that provincial child welfare authorities give their approval before a legal adoption can be completed by a court. Many authorities believe that maximum protection for all concerned is provided only when adoption placements are made through recognized child-welfare agencies.[8]

My elderly doctor in Quebec reminisced about the days before the adoption services were set up. He had a little black book wherein he would record children who would be "coming up for adoption." He would know of families who wanted children, and the match would be made. He spoke of the sense of "playing God" as he tried his best to match the children through his knowledge of the families. "We all did it," he told me. There was no other way at the time.

Along with the act of adoption came the ancient problem: the tenuous balance between the adoptive family holding specific information close to their breast, and the adopted children, told nothing but that they were adopted and intensely interested in obtaining more information. What had begun as a code of laws facilitating the movement of children from one family to another became a social problem. But not for long. The concept of sealed records was born.

There are great discrepancies in regulations concerning open records. Before 1924 all records in the United States were open. England sealed their records pertaining to adoption in 1926, but Scotland in 1930 passed a law permitting adoptees to obtain their original birth certificates once they became seventeen. Israel, in 1948, passed legislation opening the records. Two states in Australia, seventeen in the United States, New Zealand, Finland (which never had sealed-records legislation) and Sweden have recognized in law the importance of identifying information to adoptees.

There was considerable concern that adopted children, now adults, would be harmed by the knowledge of their past and that the family structure would be seriously weakened. The research of McWhinnie, Triseliotis and Rowe persuaded the majority in the British Parliament that little or no harm had resulted in Scotland where birth certificates had been released since 1930. Counselling was made a requirement for any applicant who was adopted before 1975.[9]

England finally opened its records in 1975 by section 26 of the Child Welfare Act, which

> ... empowered them [the adoptees] to gain at least some information. They were not regarded as sufficiently responsible and/or capable enough to cope with that sort of information, so special procedures involving age limits and counselling were established. The process of being adopted and growing up adopted becomes then, a process of being separated as a consequence of that status. Adoption is an experience of being different by virtue of membership of a statistically defined minority group; it is also the experience of being made marginal by a set of social processes embodied in the structural arrangements of adoption. For example: adopted children have their own, separate birth registers; there are adoption social workers who are specialists with separate offices; adoption records are kept separately; adoption clients in Children's Aid are treated separately from others.[10]

In Finland since the 1920s adoption legislation has taken into account the fact that identification may be wished at some time. The birth mother may inquire about the child, and she is told at the time of the placement that the agency will cooperate if she wishes to meet the child after she/he reaches the age of twenty. The decision to meet is up to the young adult.[11] Distinct problems do arise, and there is official recognition of the problems, but Rauteman states that adoptees should be entitled to know their background.

She points out that

> . . . by training, social workers want to protect their clients from social squalor, disease and mental illness but . . . in this kind of work, it is not possible. There is no use in trying to make things "nicer" for everyone. The only thing we can do is try to understand reality and to interpret this understanding to the client. . . . I feel that if we are able to understand that all kinds of things happen to people in life, and if we can feel compassion for them, we can tell our young clients about their background in a way that is not destructive, whatever the background may be. . . . The child's desire to know about his background may be very threatening to the adoptive parents. They also need help.[12]

The laws relating to sealed records in Canada were passed over sixty years ago. Nothing is the same as it was then. We have come so far in family counselling, in awareness of group and family dynamics, in divorce laws, in family planning — the list goes on and on — and now the law must recognize the right of the adoptee to know his true background and have access to information that may have a direct effect on his life and well being.

Notes

1. Erlich, H., *A Time to Search*, p.10.
2. Encyclopedia Britannica, Vol. 1, p.163.
3. Ibid., p.164.

4. Raynor, L., *The Adopted Child Comes of Age*, p.60.
5. Erlich, H., p.11.
6. Ibid., p.13.
7. Encyclopedia Canadiana, Vol. 2, p.352.
8. Ibid., p.353.
9. Garber, R., p.39.
10. Haimes, *Adoption, Identity and Social Policy*, p.80.
11. Ibid., pp.24, 25
12. Ibid., p.25.

BIBLIOGRAPHY

AIGNER, HAL
1987 *Faint Trails: A Guide to Adult Adoptee-Birth Parent Reunification Searches.* Greenbrae, CA: Paradigm.

ALLEN, HELEN
1982 *Today's Child.* Toronto: Ontario Ministry of Social Services.

ANSFIELD, JOSEPH G.
1971 *The Adopted Child.* Springfield, IL: Charles C. Thomas.

BOHMAN, MICHAEL
1970 *Adopted Children and Their Families.* Stockholm: Proprius Press.

BRIDGES, WILLIAM
1980 *Transitions.* Reading, MA: Addison-Wesley.

BURGESS, LINDA CANNON
1976 *The Art of Adoption.* New York, London: Norton. Toronto: George J. McLeod.

CARSE, JAMES P.
1986 *Finite and Infinite Games: A Vision of Life as Play and Possibility.* New York: Free Press.

ENCYCLOPEDIA BRITANNICA
1875-1889 Ninth edition. Chicago: Encyclopedia Britannica.

ENCYLOPEDIA CANADIANA
1957 Ottawa: The Canadian Company.

ERLICH, H.
    1977 *A Time to Search*. London: Paddington.
FISHER, F.
    1973 *In Search of Anna Fisher*. New York: Arthur Fields.
GARBER, RALPH
    1985 *Disclosure of Adoption Information*. Report of the Special Commissioner to the Honourable John Sweeney, Minister of Community and Social Services. Toronto: Government of Ontario. November.
GIDDENS, LYNN
    1983 *Faces of Adoption*. Chapel Hills, NC: Amberley.
HAIMES, ERICA and NOEL TIMMS
    1985 *Adoption, Identity, and Social Policy*. London: Gower
JAFFEE, BENSON
    1974 "Adoptive Outcome: A Two Generation View." *Child Welfare U.S.A.* Volume 53, Number 4.
JAFFEE, BENSON and DAVID FANSHEL
    1970 *How They Fared in Adoption: A Follow-up Study*. New York and London: Columbia University Press.
KORNITZER, MARGARET
    1968 *Adoption and Family Life*. London: Putnam.
LIFTON, BETTY JEAN
    1978 *Lost and Found: The Adoption Experience*. New York: Dial.
McWHINNIE, A.M.
    1967 *Adopted Children - How They Grow Up: A Study of Their Adjustment as Adults*. London: Routledge and Kegan. New York: Humanities Press.
MANDELL, BETTY REID
    1973 *Where Are the Children?* Lexington, Toronto, London: D.C. Heath.
MARCUS, CLARE
    1979 *Adopted? A Canadian Guide for Adopted Adults in*

Search of Their Origins. Vancouver, Toronto, Seattle: International Self-Counsel Press.

1981 *Who Is My Mother?* Toronto: Macmillan.

MARSHALL, JOAN

1990 *How to Search in Canada.* Nepean, ON: Searchline.

ONTARIO MINISTRY OF COMMUNITY AND SOCIAL SERVICES

1983 *The Child and Family Services Act: Draft Legislation and Background Paper.* Toronto: Ontario Ministry of Community and Social Services. November.

RAYNOR, LOIS

1980 *The Adopted Child Comes of Age.* London: G.A. Unwin

ROSNER, GERTRUDE

1961 *Crisis of Self Doubt.* New York: Child Welfare League.

SANDNESS, GRACE

◄ 1984 *Commitment: The Reality of Adoption.* Maple Grove, MN: Mini World Publications.

SEGLOW, JEAN, MIA-LILLY PRINGLE and PETER WEDGE

1972 *Growing Up Adopted: A Report by the National Children's Bureau.* London: National Institute for Educational Research in England and Wales.

SHAWYER, JOSS

1979 *Death by Adoption.* Auckland, New Zealand: Cicada.

SILVERMAN, PHYLLIS R., LEE CAMPBELL, PATRICIA STYLE and CAROLYN BRIGGS

1988 "Reunions between Adoptees and Birth Parents: The Birth Parents' Experience." *Social Work.* Nov.-Dec.

SOROSKY, A.D., ANNETTE BARON and RUBEN PANNER

1984 *The Adoption Triangle: The Effect of Sealed Records.* New York: Anchor.

SWEENEY, JOHN

1986 *Ontario's New Adoption Disclosure Policy.* Toronto: Ontario Ministry of Community and Social Services. June.

TRISELIOTIS, JOHN
1973 *Adoptees in Search of Their Origins*. Edinborough: Edinborough University Press.

WILLIAMS, MARGERY
1991 *The Velveteen Rabbit*. Garden City, New York: Doubleday.